CHAPEL
USP CANAAN

Manners
Made Easy
FOR THE FAMILY

Manners Made Easy

FOR THE FAMILY

365 Timeless Etiquette Tips
for Every Occasion

June Hines Moore

PUBLISHING GROUP

Nashville, Tennessee

ISBN: 978-0-8054-4741-5
B & H Publishing Group
Nashville, Tennessee
www.BHPublishingGroup.com

Dewey Decimal Classification: 395
Manners and Customs / Etiquette / Family Life

Interior illustrations by Abe Goolsby

Printed in the USA
1 2 3 4 5 6 7   12 11 10 09 08

Dedication

To my husband, Homer,
who is my greatest inspiration.

To my family,
Greg, Jeff, Leslie, Laura Beth, and Mary Cate.

To all the students I have had the privilege to teach.

With special recognition to my computer tech,
Tim Joiner, who serves as my brain and my hands
when mine refuse to solve my computer problems,
which are legion at times.

We put rules of etiquette in our head
and manners in our heart.

The rules guide our behavior and keep
us from embarrassing ourselves.

The manners in our heart keep us from
embarrassing someone else.

Table of Contents

Introduction

Part One: Meeting and Greeting 1–31

Part Two: Making Introductions 32–54

Part Three: Telephone Manners 55–84

Part Four: The Perfect Guest 85–112

Part Five: The Gracious Host 113–126

Part Six: Church Manners 127–148

Part Seven: Electronic Etiquette 149–166

Part Eight: The Words We Say 167–189

Part Nine: Public Manners and Traveling 190–221

Part Ten: Notes And Letters 222–247

Part Eleven: Fine Dining 248–348

Part Twelve: Other Good Manners 349–366

31 Days to Good Manners

Index

Introduction

Manners Were God's Idea First

Every member of every family has manners—good or bad. Our good manners show consideration for the feelings of others, while our bad ones reveal thoughtlessness and rudeness. We can't touch them or see them. We get our manners by default, but not by birth. Even members of the royal family must learn good manners.

But if we can't touch or see them and we are not born with them, then where did they come from? Manners were God's idea first.

All manners, both socially and in business, are based on the Bible, especially on Luke 6:31 where God gave us the Golden Rule: *Do for others as you would like them to do for you*. From this beginning, manners touch everything we do in life.

If you have ever dined with a two-year-old, for example, you know why we have table manners. As one of my young students said, "It's so we don't gross somebody out." Truth is, we learn our manners at home from our families. And just as we do not send out our family without rules of safety, such as "walk facing traffic," we do not want them to go out with bad manners (and maybe not even know it).

Good manners are more than knowing which fork to use or which way to pass food around the table. There are the etiquette rules and reasons that go in our head, and there are the manners that go in our heart. Together they give us a shield against embarrassing others or ourselves.

The CEO of a major corporation invited me to teach a business etiquette seminar to his employees. "Mrs. Moore," he said, "we surely do need more eta-kwet taught." I used to teach French (*etiquette* is a French word we Americans have adopted) and now I teach etiquette (pronounced et-i-ket). You can imagine how badly I wanted to correct him, but my doing so would have embarrassed him. I had the rules of pronunciation in my head, but the manners in my heart kept me from correcting him.

Whether this book is just a manners catch-up for your family or a full blown course in social skills, learning the rules of etiquette can give us new-found confidence. Sometimes I hear people averse to learning manners say, "Oh, I know the correct thing to do when I have to." But the truth is, they only *know* of it. Unless we do something habitually, we have what we call "company manners," which are likely to fail us when we need them most. We become self-conscious and usually forget what, how, and when to do the correct thing the very moment we need to do it. Even if we suddenly remember, we fumble, stumble, and sometimes look foolish trying to pull it off.

Most of us like to know the reason for doing something, and there is a sound reason for every rule of etiquette. I mentioned one earlier: for reasons of safety, we walk facing traffic. Another reason is related to how we meet and greet people in our country, not with a kiss, as in some cultures, but with a handshake. Our country was settled by men who carried weapons. To show they were a friend, not an enemy, they extended their open hand. The natural result was our handshake greeting.

For those family members who are reluctant to begin "etiquette class," be encouraged: just going through the motions can create some good social habits. The heartfelt kind will come along later when they see how necessary good people skills are for the rest of their lives in relationships and in the business world. Our behavior affects it all. Our manners make us like magnets. We either attract people or repel them.

In summary: We put rules of etiquette in our head, and we put manners in our heart. The rules in our head guide our behavior and keep us from embarrassing ourselves. The manners in our heart keep us from embarrassing someone else.

I admire your desire for more mannerly families. Here's to happy learning and happier living!

June Hines Moore
2008

Part I
Meeting and Greeting

Respect for ourselves guides our morals;
respect for others guides our manners.
—*Laurence Sterne*

First Things First

Making a good first impression is a worthy goal for two reasons: 1) there is no second chance, and 2) it only takes a few seconds. We are blessed, of course, that God looks at our heart, but people form their opinion of us in the first thirty seconds by judging our appearance, our visual communication, and our manners. They evaluate our inner qualities later.

Suggestion: Memorize the **six S's**, and in the following days, you will be well equipped to confidently meet and greet people. The six S's are 1) **Stand** up, 2) **Smile**, 3) **See** their eyes, 4) **Shake** hands, 5) **Speak** your name, and 6) **Say** their name back to them. Why not see who in the family can memorize the six S's first?

Man does not see what the Lord sees, for man sees what is visible, but the Lord sees the heart.
1 Samuel 16:7

Stand on Principle

The first "S" in the six S's of making a good impression is *Stand up*. When you (either an adult or child) are meeting someone for the first time, stand up if that person is standing. (Exception: Sometimes it is not practical or even possible to stand. In that case, just let common sense dictate.) Standing puts you at eye level with the other person and, more importantly, it shows respect.

In today's casual world, first impressions have never been more important. Standing to greet another person will make you stand out in a crowd.

Suggestion: Practice rising from a chair to meet someone who's just entered the room.

The two angels entered Sodom in the evening as Lot was sitting at Sodom's gate. When Lot saw them, he got up to meet them.
Genesis 19:1

Children Showing Honor

Children are to stand up for any adult they are meeting, as well as any time an adult walks into the room. Children should always defer (show honor) to adults. George Washington's *Rules of Civility*, which he copied down when he was sixteen, said, "If any one comes to Speak to you while you are Sitting, Stand up."

Children are more highly regarded when they show respect to adults. Only gentle reminders by other members of the family should be permitted when a young person forgets.

Suggestion: While sitting in the family room, practice standing every time a parent (or other adult) walks into the room. Discuss what honor and respect mean, especially in today's culture.

Teach a youth about the way he should go;
even when he is old he will not depart from it.
Proverbs 22:6

All Rise

Men should stand up when a lady enters (or when ladies enter) a room. Socially, a gentleman defers (shows honor and respect) to a woman. A long, time-honored custom in our country says men should stand for adult females.

A similar custom comes from the Middle Ages, when knights wore metal shields over their heads. They lifted the head covering to expose their eyes, showing they were friendly, thus the tradition behind a man tipping his hat or touching the brim when he sees a lady.

Suggestion: Let Dad practice standing when a female member of the family enters the room. (Only a gentle reminder is permitted when Dad forgets). Name as many people or categories of people you can who deserve your honor and respect.

✦ ✦ ✦ ✦ ✦ ✦ ✦

Honor everyone.
1 Peter 2:17

Table Legs

Gentlemen should stand when a lady gets up from a dining table, and stand again when she returns. Upon her return, the man nearest her should help her with the chair as she is reseated.

Chairs are not as difficult to maneuver these days as they once were when this act became common courtesy, but still, as a time-honored tradition, gentlemen should help to seat ladies at the table.

Suggestion: Let Dad and the young men of the family practice pulling out a chair and seating each lady in the family. Also, look up the word "humility." What is its meaning? Give examples of ways to show humility (not being prideful, boastful, or self-asserting).

The fear of the Lord is wisdom's instruction,
and humility comes before honor.
Proverbs 15:33

Age Preference

Men aren't the only ones with a responsibility to stand in certain social situations. Adult women and young ladies should also stand for any person who is much older than they. In our society, younger individuals honor older ones, whether male or female.

Suggestion: This time, it is the ladies' turn. Let the daughters in the family practice standing when Mom or Dad enter the room. If Grandmother is there, all the ladies in the family (as well as the men and boys) should rise when she enters the room. Discuss how humility and conceit are different in meaning, with conceit meaning self-importance.

Good manners alone won't guarantee your entrance to today's boardrooms, but without good manners the doors to many chambers will be closed to you forever.

Anonymous

I Want to See You Smile

The second "S" in making a good first impression is *Smile*. When meeting someone for the first time and any time thereafter, give them a smile. When you meet someone not wearing a smile, give them one of yours.

Everyone likes to be greeted with a warm smile, and a smile is the same in any language. An old adage says, "If you are happy, notify your face." After all, it takes only fourteen muscles to smile but more than seventy to frown.

Suggestion: Practice smiling when you speak to members of your family.

Having good manners means doing with a smile what you have to do anyway.

Anonymous

Look into My Eyes

The third "S" in making a good first impression is *See their eyes*. We usually say "make eye contact" or "look people in the eye." When we do, we show that we care enough to give them our full attention. Notice, you must look into other people's faces to see their smile.

Suggestion: If you have difficulty looking people in the eye, practice in front of a mirror. Look into a mirror and say, "Hello, how are you?" being careful to continue looking into your eyes, not down or to the side. You may feel silly at first, but it will become easier with practice.

Your eye is the lamp of the body. When your eye is good, your whole body is also full of light.
Luke 11:34

All-Around Attention

The eyes have often been called "the window to the soul." But sometimes it can feel awkward to stay focused on someone's eyes when speaking to him. If you are uncomfortable looking people in the eye, try looking from their eyes to their mouth, then back to their eyes. Remember, you're not staring unless you look into someone's eyes without blinking or looking away.

Suggestion: If you have trouble looking people in the eye, practice this technique: look around their face, but never away from it. Have fun trying this with each other as a family.

Let your countenance be pleasant.
George Washington

A Fair Shake

The fourth "S" in making a good first impression is *Shake the other person's hand* with a firm but not crushing handclasp.

Americans shake hands because our country was settled by men who carried weapons for protection. If a man wanted to show he was a friend and not an enemy, he would extend his open, gun-free hand to the other. This gesture is where the handshake was born. (Ladies offered their hand for gentlemen to kiss in pioneer America.)

Suggestion: Practice shaking hands with each family member. Check for firmness and for a grasp that meets the web of each other's hand between the thumb and first finger.

No one cares which way your pinkie is pointing when your heart is going in the right direction.

Anonymous

The Proper Handshake

Men and women both shake hands the same way—firm, but not crushing—and women shake hands with both women and men.

A woman should extend her right hand with the thumb pointing upward. She should not offer her fingers only (in a flat, turned-down-palm position) to anyone for a handshake, because it is very difficult for a gentleman to grasp a lady's hand for a handshake unless she offers her whole hand properly.

Suggestion: Practice extending your right hand with the thumb upward and the little finger downward, sliding the web between your thumb and forefinger to meet the web of the other person's hand, giving a firm grasp.

*Handshakes are the physical greetings
that go with your words.*

Anonymous

Should I Shake Her Hand?

In our early pioneer days, women did not shake hands at all. A man kissed a lady's hand, which she offered palm-down. Today, however, a lady should extend her right hand first to put a gentleman at ease. (In business, men and women extend their hand at the same time. In social situations, a man should wait for the lady to extend her hand.)

A good handshake lasts only a few seconds with a few gentle ups and downs. Either person may release the grasp first. Some people are uncomfortable holding hands for an extended time.

Suggestion: Practice shaking hands—the men waiting for the ladies to extend their right hands first as in a social situation.

No one likes the hard, pump-handle handshake.
Arthur Schlesinger

Left Alone

When one of the two individuals shaking hands has a crippled or arthritic right hand, the healthy left hand is often extended. So shake the hand you are offered. Usually, the individual with an impaired right hand wishes to shake hands in his or her own way. Be sensitive to his or her preferences.

Others are naturally much more sensitive to their own special circumstances and limitations than you are. Try making them comfortable and at ease with you as quickly as possible.

Suggestion: Have one family member pretend to have his or her right arm in a sling. If you are the individual with no impairment, extend your right hand and grasp the left hand extended to you.

[Jesus] told the man with the paralyzed hand,
"Get up and stand here. . . . Stretch out your hand."
Luke 6:8, 10

A Word of Explanation

If you are unable or do not wish to shake hands, keep your hands behind you, out of sight. Others are uncomfortable and not immediately sure how to react when their offer of a handshake is rejected. If your hands are out of sight, the greeter more readily knows not to offer his hand to begin with.

Suggestion: Practice what to say if you are unable to shake hands: "You won't mind if I don't shake hands; I have a bad case of arthritis," or simply say, "Sorry, I can't shake hands." By explaining this upfront, you put the other person at ease and avoid embarrassment for both of you.

For we do not have a high priest who is unable to sympathize with our weaknesses.
Hebrews 4:15

Cold Hands, Warm Heart

Handshakes are important even if you have cold hands or sweaty palms, because it is always awkward when a person extends his hand and the other person does not offer his or hers in return. Other people usually do not even notice these sensations or consider them to be as disagreeable as we fear they will. Better to greet people warmly, even with cold hands. As Emily Kimbrough said, "Remember, we all stumble, every one of us. That's why it's a comfort to go hand in hand."

Suggestion: Practice wiping your right hand on your clothes before you extend it. Say, "Please excuse my cold (or wet) hand."

*O, would that we could see ourselves
as others see us.*
Robert Burns

Hello, My Name Is . . .

The fifth "S" in making a good first impression is *Speak your name*. Introduce yourself, saying your first and last names slowly and distinctly.

If we run our first and last names together, such as Maryanndrews, it is difficult to understand. Is it Mary Andrews or Mary Ann Drews? If you say, "My name is Mary Ann (slight pause) Drews," or "Mary (pause) Andrews," your new friend will more easily understand you.

Suggestion: Practice saying your first and last names slowly and distinctly. Have family members give gentle critiques.

The Lord said to [Moses], "Who made the human mouth? . . . I will help you speak and I will teach you what to say."
Exodus 4:11–12

Hello to You, Too

The sixth "S" in making a good first impression is *Say the person's name back*. After the other person tells you her name, you should repeat the name back, saying, "Hello, Mary Ann (or Mrs. Drews)."

There are three benefits to repeating the name back: 1) it makes the name easier for you to remember, 2) you can make sure you are pronouncing the name correctly, and 3) people simply like to hear their name spoken.

Suggestion: Let another family member choose a "pretend" name and then introduce himself or herself to you. If you do not understand the name, say, "I'm sorry, could you say your name again, please?" (or something similar).

Knowledge speaks, but wisdom listens.
Jimi Hendrix

Getting to Know You

If someone does not introduce himself at first, you should introduce yourself and then ask his name. Do not wait long into your conversation to do this. Perhaps the other person thinks you already know his name or (more likely) he just doesn't know the six S's very well!

Suggestion: Pretend you are with strangers. Have each family member in turn simply begin talking without giving their names. You can say, "Hi, my name is Tom Nichols (substitute your name). May I ask yours?" It's fun to do this with a neighbor or group of friends.

In 1600 America, people were punished in public for name-calling, cursing, scandalmongering, and making ugly faces.
Arthur Schlesinger

R-E-S-P-E-C-T

Young people should be taught to use an adult's title by saying Dr., Reverend, Mr., Ms., or Mrs., and a last name to show respect. Children who are well-taught in these kinds of simple courtesies show self-confidence, maturity, and interest in other people.

Suggestion: Practice with these various examples of meeting: 1) As a parent, when you and your child approach an adult friend, introduce your child to your friend, making sure your child addresses the other adult by title and last name. 2) Practice the six S's at family reunions. 3) When playmates come over, let younger members of the family introduce their guests to you, and you to them.

Just as the twig is bent, the tree's inclin'd.
Alexander Pope

Hesitation in Your Voice

When meeting a new acquaintance, a very shy child should smile, nod, and try very hard to look him in the eye. It may be too uncomfortable for the child to shake hands and talk to a new person until he or she first learns to smile and nod.

Margaret Visser's *Rituals of Dinner* states, "Until children are between two and four years old, they know fear and shyness, but they do not blush or cringe or react in other bodily ways to social faux pas."

Suggestion: Encourage family members to practice the six S's. Modeling the proper procedure will teach more than the "manners police" can.

Home is where children learn 95 percent of the things they take with them into life.

Thomas Armstrong

Different Strokes, Different Folks

It is always good manners to take each person's temperament and feelings into consideration when learning and practicing rules of etiquette. People are born with different personalities. Some are outgoing and friendly from their infancy. Others are shy, reserved, and perhaps easily intimidated.

Suggestion: For young, very shy members of the family, it is fun to practice meeting and greeting with a teddy bear or a doll. High-energy, sociable family members may need to exercise patience while other members learn and practice.

When the boys grew up, Esau became an expert hunter, an outdoorsman, but Jacob was a quiet man who stayed at home.
Genesis 25:27

The First Twelve Inches

The first twelve inches above and below our shoulders should be impeccable. So to make a good impression, we must observe rules such as those concerning the way we walk, stand, and appear in our clothes.

People look at our overall appearance to form their impressions. If we have a dab of mustard on our mouth, or hair and lint on our shoulders, the impression we give may not be the best.

Suggestion: Check your appearance often in a mirror, especially your head and shoulders. Family members may give gentle critiques since they can see you more easily than you can see yourself without a mirror.

Show nothing to your friend that may affright him.
George Washington

Straight Ahead

To make a good impression, we must walk confidently while looking straight ahead, as if we have a destination. Taking baby steps and looking at the ground as we walk makes us look introverted, timid, and insecure.

Suggestion: Practice walking in front of a mirror or store windows to observe yourself. One fun activity for the family is to critique actors in movies or on television, being very careful never to actually judge people we know.

Jesus spoke to them again: "I am the light of the world. Anyone who follows Me will never walk in the darkness but will have the light of life."

John 8:12

Up to the Task

To make a positive impression and show confidence (not arrogance), we must stand erect and walk with our chin level to the floor, holding our shoulders up. Otherwise we may appear lazy, tired, or indifferent. If we drop our chin, we cannot look people in the eye. If we point our nose in the air, we look aloof, disinterested, or self-centered.

Suggestion: Pretend you have a string attached to your breastbone, with someone above pulling the string. The torso rises with an imaginary pull upward, pulling in the midriff but not throwing the shoulders out of line. You may also check your posture in your shadow.

A judge in New Orleans declared a mistrial and ruled that the plaintiff's attorney prejudiced the jury merely through eye contact and body language.

Associated Press

Base of Operations

Shoes should always be kept clean and in good repair, because people look down at our shoes even though we may not notice. Scuffed, rundown footwear makes us look careless, inattentive to detail.

Interestingly, in the Far East, the removal of shoes while indoors means that the guest is disarming himself, showing respect, and making himself similar to the host, who is also shoeless.

Suggestion: Check often to see if the heels and soles on your shoes need replacing. Make sure your shoestrings are taut and intact. All your shoes should be washed, clean, or polished, whatever is applicable to each pair.

In Oxford, Ohio, there is a law against wearing patent leather shoes.

The Way You Look Tonight

The way we dress should not produce unpleasant reactions or feelings in others. If we dress appropriately, we show respect for the ones who have to look at us. People prefer that we don't shock them with our attire—or with our lack of it! Our appearance often reveals our self-respect.

Suggestion: Let each family member give a verbal description of disrespectful attire—both in adults as well as children and teenagers. Talk about why respect for others is more important than our own personal preferences or comfort.

The critical factor in credibility is presenting the expected image. Don't wear anything that will surprise the people you meet.

John Molloy

Pretty in Private

Never comb your hair or use toothpicks or dental floss in public. Doing so is unsightly and exposes others to germs or to a stray hair in food. Practices of personal hygiene should be done in private, not at the table or in other public settings where they're noticeable and unbecoming. Working hard not to offend or unsettle others by your actions is a form of showing respect.

Suggestion: Family members can practice combing their hair and washing their hands before sitting down to eat. After a while, doing so should become a good habit.

*Keep your nails clean and short,
also your hands and teeth clean, yet without
showing any great concern for them.*
George Washington

Pick-Up Patrol

A secondary rule of good grooming is to clean up after ourselves before leaving the bathroom. In a family setting, those we love are sure to use the bathroom after us, and they deserve our respect. Even in public bathrooms, be thoughtful of others by wiping up any spills or splatters after washing your hands at the sink.

Suggestion: Provide a towel rack, drawer, tray, or whatever is necessary for members of the family to organize their toiletries. If each family member cleans up after himself, the bathroom stays neat and tidy for the next parent, sibling, or guest to use.

It's the law in Bare, Vermont, that everyone must take a bath on Saturday night.

All Hands on Deck

To make a good impression, we should keep our hands in sight because when our hands are hidden from view, such as when stuffed into a pocket, we appear sneaky, insecure, or self-conscious. Work at getting more comfortable in public without having your hands tucked in a pocket or belt loop or held behind your back. It will make you appear more approachable and at ease.

Suggestion: Practice walking and standing while keeping your hands out of your pockets (unless you must quickly retrieve something).

When in company, put not your hands to any part of the body not usually discovered.
George Washington

Relax Yourself

The proper way to stand is with the arms free and relaxed, hanging at our sides. If we cross our arms across our chest, tucking our hands under our arms, we appear to be cold, mad, or indifferent. Similarly, holding our hands below our waist, clasping our hands so our arms form a "v," droops the shoulders and presents us in an unflattering pose.

Suggestion: To appear warm and approachable, practice walking and standing with your arms hanging loosely at your sides. It honestly looks much more natural than it may feel to you.

Let your carriage be such as becomes a man grave, settled and attentive to that which is spoken.
George Washington

Common Scents

Perfume and cologne should whisper, not shout. Some people are allergic to the aromas given off by our well-chosen fragrance. While we may enjoy the aroma ourself, others may become ill.

This courtesy quietly expresses our respect and sensitivity toward others. It's also a reminder that striking a good first impression is often a matter of keeping yourself from being overly noticeable.

Suggestion: Discuss your perfume, cologne, or after shave with others to see if it's too strong. Sometimes just a little goes a long way. Since we can become immune to scents, it may be a good idea to ask friends or coworkers to give their opinion.

Wear not your clothes foul or ripped but see they be brushed once every day and take heed that you approach not to any uncleanness.
George Washington

Part 2
Making Introductions

Anyone can be polite to a king.
It takes a gentleman to be polite to a beggar.

Anonymous

For Starters

Introducing one person to another or to several persons is one of the most important rules of good manners. An introduction is simply sharing a friend's name with another friend or acquaintance so the two of them can talk comfortably.

Perhaps the most important rule of making introductions is to make the effort even when we cannot remember the names (see #34). People appreciate it more than we realize.

Suggestion: As a family, discuss how it makes you feel when you are with a friend you know well, another person unknown to you walks up, and your friend fails to introduce you. Talk about how to use the six S's when that happens.

He first found his own brother Simon . . .
and he brought Simon to Jesus.
John 1:41–42

Names, Please

Knowing how to introduce people gives us confidence, new friendships, as well as the opportunity to make a good impression. Therefore, children and parents alike must not neglect to introduce one another in social settings.

Suggestion: Gather some hats or caps to practice making introductions over the next few days. For instance, one child can wear the ball cap of a young athlete, and the other child can wear a referee's cap. The player wearing the ball cap will be introduced to the referee because the younger is always introduced to the older.

* ♦ * ♦ * ♦ * ♦ * ♦

*Giving a friend's name to another friend
is like giving him or her a present—the gift
of knowing one another.*
Anonymous

Important Matters

Here are the rules of introductions: Decide first who is more important in respect to age or gender (older over younger, female over male). Address the more important first, speaking the first and last names of this person. Next, speak the first and last names of the less important person: "Laura Danmire, this is my friend Jay Ingalls." Then give some information that will easily launch both of them into conversation: "Jay knows your brother Stu from Boy Scouts."

Suggestion: By passing around hats and caps, choose the most important person. Mary (female) is more important than John (male). Your grandfather is more important than young Suzie—age over gender. Practice introducing them in the proper order.

Be an example to the believers in speech,
in conduct, in love, in faith, in purity.
1 Timothy 4:12

Don't Assume First Names

If at all unsure, never assume that you can use first names alone when addressing or introducing someone. You can never go wrong using a title and someone's last name—"Mr. Neal" instead of just "Larry."

It's also important to give both the first and last names in an introduction. If you don't know the first name, use only the title and last name.

Suggestion: Pretend you are unsure about calling a person by his first name, so you use his last name, such as Mr. Smith. If he doesn't expect to be treated so formally, Mr. Smith can always tell you to just call him John.

* ♦ ♦ ♦ ♦ ♦

Likewise, you younger men,
be subject to the elders.
1 Peter 5:5

Wait, I Know You

If you find it impossible to remember the name of one of the friends when making an introduction, you may say the name of the friend you do remember. Usually, the other person involved will make a self-introduction, making everyone more comfortable.

Suggestion: Practicing the above rule is more fun if you invite outsiders to join in. Ask two friends over to your house. Pretend to forget the name of one of the friends. Look in the face of the friend whose name has escaped you and say, "I don't think you've met Joey Webb, my friend from church." The friend with the elusive name will probably say, "Hi, Joey. I'm Mel Innis." Then Joey says, "Hi, Mel." They shake hands and you breathe a sigh of relief.

Bring them up in the training and
instruction of the Lord.
Ephesians 6:4

Ladies First

In making introductions, we must understand the issue of "importance." Again, importance refers to the way we show respect in matters of etiquette, based simply on age and gender.

After you decide the most important person between the two individuals you are introducing, you should look at that person first. By doing so, you are recognizing that this person is the first line of honor. Deliberately turning to this person is also a reminder to yourself that you should speak his or her name first, then introduce the other person, not the other way around.

Suggestion: Have one of the children look at Mom (female) and introduce a younger family member. For instance, "Mom, this is Susan, my friend" or "Granddad, this is my classmate, Jerry."

Nothing is so strong as gentleness,
nothing so gentle as strength.
Francis of Assisi

You're Nice to Say

Today is practice day. Remember again the rules of importance: introduce a male to a female, a younger person to an older person. Then try to make some point of connection or conversation starter.

Suggestion: Practice by having one family member say to another, "Mary Jones, this is John Dailey." You honor Mary by introducing the young man to her. Then turn and say, "John, this is Mary Jones. She's a friend of mine from school."

Now practice based on age: "Mrs. Appleby, this is my friend, Sam Holstead, from next door." Then turn to Sam and say, "Sam, this is Mrs. Appleby, my mom's friend from garden club." Make up other scenarios for your family to practice.

Every action done in company ought to be with some sign of respect to those that are present.
George Washington

Introductions at Work

In a professional or academic setting, introduce a less important person in rank to a higher-ranking individual—employee to the CEO, the CEO to any customer or client—because in business, we show respect to the person in a higher position. This generally takes precedence over the male-to-female or younger-to-older distinctions.

Suggestion: Practice by saying, "Mr. Wingate (boss), this is our new associate, Miss Evie Marks." Then turn to Miss Marks and give her the complete name of the boss: "Evie, this is Gerald Wingate, our director of sales" (along with any special titles such as Dr. or CEO). She needs the last name because she would not want to call him Gerald.

* ♦ ♦ ♦ ♦ ♦ ♦

Manners are not idle, but the fruit of loyal nature and of noble mind.
Alfred, Lord Tennyson

When in Doubt

Sometimes when we need to make an introduction, we are not sure who should receive the most respect or honor because we don't know which person is older or is in a higher-ranking position. We must try to introduce the two people just the same. It is bad manners to ignore making an introduction.

Suggestion: Practice by using two gentlemen's names or the names of two ladies in the same generation. For instance, say, "Jim Bain, this is Phil Grimes, my partner at work," or a student can say, "Kevin, this is my teammate, Bill Stewart" then "Bill, this is my friend, Kevin Knight." The order of the names is not important in this instance.

It costs nothing to be polite.
Winston Churchill

Honored Guests

When introducing a family member, honor the non-related person by looking at him or her first, because we honor guests or those outside our family by presenting our family members to them.

Introductions can also be contextual, based on the circumstances. For instance, our U.S. president becomes the honored guest when he is in England, whereas the prime minister of England is the honored guest when visiting our country. They are equal in dignity and importance worldwide, but each is honored in the homeland of the other dignitary.

Suggestion: Pretend your name is Brian Harvey. Introduce your mom to your coach. Say, "Coach Adamson, this is my mother, Barbara Harvey" and then "Mom, meet Coach Adamson."

Good social skills are truly an equalizer. They transcend racial and socio-economic differences.

Anonymous

Making Connections

It's always helpful to know something about the person we are meeting so we can make good conversation. When introducing people, try to give each individual a little information about the other one. By doing so, we help our friends move past the first awkward moments of meeting.

Suggestion: Practice by saying, "Mrs. Casey, this is my mom." Then, "Mom, this is Mrs. Casey, our new music teacher." This way, Mrs. Casey might say something nice about you to your mom, and your mom can welcome Mrs. Casey, who is new to the school or community.

*Good nature is more agreeable
in conversation than wit.*
Joseph Addison

Looking Here, Looking There

When making a person-to-person introduction, look at the person who needs the new information before turning to the other. You should not tell someone his own name by looking at him when you say it, because it is difficult to hear the name if the introducer is looking away from you when you say it.

Suggestion: For practice, pretend you're looking at a friend, and give her your other friend's name. "Angela, this is Keith Lamb, our new neighbor." Then turn to Keith and say, "Keith, Angela has been my friend since first grade." The important thing here is to look at the person who needs the information or the new name.

Learning the rules of etiquette coupled with good manners in our heart helps us operate smoothly within the social code.

Anonymous

Filler Words

When making an introduction, don't just repeat the names like a bouncing ball. It sounds awkward to say, "Mrs. Jones, Ms. Smith. Ms. Smith, Mrs. Jones," especially when we are standing quite close to someone in a quiet environment. Fill the space between each person's name by inserting some appropriate words of introduction.

Suggestion: For practice, try this introduction: "Mrs. Jones, I'd like to introduce Ms. Smith." The two women are within close proximity to you and to one another. Just make sure each lady can hear the name of the other one by facing the one who needs the information.

Manners must adorn knowledge,
and smooth its way through the world.
Lord Chesterfield

Pleasant, Not Prickly

When you are the one being introduced, always respond with a word of greeting along with the new acquaintance's name. Everyone likes to hear his name spoken by a new acquaintance.

A delightful old German fable tells of a group of porcupines, massed together against the cold, who found that they froze when too far apart and pricked each other when too close together. When they finally worked out the exact degree of proximity that kept them both warm and unstabbed, they called it good manners.

Suggestion: After practicing introductions, say: "Hello, Sam," or "How are you, Sam?" or "Good to meet you, Sam," or something similar. Remember to express a greeting and say the new friend's name back to him or her.

Conversation is one of the greatest pleasures in life.
William Somerset Maugham

The Better to Remember You

As alluded to in the previous entry, always repeat the name of a person you are meeting or have just met. While there are many good reasons for this, one of the most practical reasons to repeat the name is to help you remember it. Much of our difficulty in recalling names comes from not using them enough.

Suggestion: For practice, let each family member respond to each other member by greeting and saying the name of that family member, for example, "Hello, Mr. Humphrey. It's so nice to meet you." This activity is more fun with friends or neighbors.

Good name in man and woman . . .
is the immediate jewel of their souls.
William Shakespeare

Did I Hear You Right?

The next several tips are related to remembering names—a problem many of us struggle with. Sometimes we think it's hopeless to even try. It's not!

One of the things that often happens when we are introduced to someone is we don't quite understand what the person said his name was. Repeating the name not only helps in remembering it, but also confirms that we are pronouncing it correctly. New friends want to know that we got their name right.

Suggestion: Pretend you thought the name was Sarcowsky, but it was really BARcowsky. Repeat it back to him or her incorrectly, so that the other person can gently say, "No, it's Barcowsky." For fun, try this with other names, letting each family member take a turn.

Your test as a listener comes when you measure how much you learn from others.
Anonymous

I Say Again

Another guard against forgetting names is not only to say the person's name one time in response to the initial introduction, but also to work his or her name into several more thoughts, statements, or questions as you continue talking.

Repeating a name once after you hear it and then using it in subsequent conversation is the best insurance against forgetfulness. As a wise college professor once said, "If we use a word or a name five times, we can claim it as ours."

Suggestion: Say, "Hello, John. It's nice to meet you." Then, begin making small talk by asking, "John, have you lived here long?" or something similar. When leaving, you can say, "John, it was nice visiting with you." Repeating his name will help you remember both John and his name.

Nothing is stronger than habit.
Ovid

Names and Faces

When you do forget a name, it is proper to simply admit it. Ignoring people or failing to introduce them is far worse than having to ask them to repeat their name. It actually shows we care when we ask someone's name, even if we are supposed to know it.

Suggestion: For practice, choose a family member or friend and simply say, "I'm sorry. I know we've met, but I can't even seem to remember my own name today (or something similar). You'll have to help me out." or "Please refresh my memory of your name." Come up with your own best way of expressing this.

A polite person is polished
(from the French word "poli").

Doing the Backstroke

When someone approaches you, and you cannot remember his or her name, you can try to get the name by simply re-introducing yourself. Sometimes that individual will state his or her name after you say yours, without your having to ask for it.

Then be sure to employ the repeating techniques we talked about earlier to keep from facing this same situation with the same person again.

Suggestion: Choose a family member or friend and say, "Hi there," then give your name. Put your hand out to shake hands, hoping the other individual will reintroduce himself or herself.

To one that is your equal, or not much inferior,
you are to give the chief place in your lodging.
George Washington

Little Reminders

When you find it difficult to remember others' names, it is proper to apply the following method: When you meet a new person, try to identify something about his or her name that sticks with you as a mental image. For instance, if your friend's name is Mrs. Ringgold, you might identify her name with an earring. (The danger here is calling the friend Mrs. Earring, but it works for some people.)

Suggestion: For practice (and fun), look at each family member and try to associate their name with something about them. Only clean and kind names are allowed, of course, for this name association technique.

♦ ♦ ♦ ♦ ♦ ♦ ♦

When I am introduced to one,
I wish I thought, "What jolly fun!"
Sir Walter Raleigh

That's Not Me

It is proper to make a one-time correction of the pronunciation of your name if others mispronounce it. No one does so intentionally, and the offender will usually thank you for the correction, even if it creates a slight bit of embarrassment or awkwardness. Never feel as though you're being rude about correcting the pronunciation of your name.

Suggestion: Try intentionally mispronouncing a family member's name, then say it correctly after you are reminded. Pretend, for example, that your name is Alissa. When your family member says "Hello, Melissa," you can simply say, "It's Alissa."

When you realize you have made a mistake, make amends immediately. It is easier to eat crow while it's still warm.
Dan Heist

Group Dynamics

If you find yourself in a group when a friend or acquaintance walks up, you should introduce the new person to the group. It's not that hard. There's an easy way to do it. Simply say the new person's name to the group of five or more ("Guys, this is Brad"), and then let them introduce themselves one by one, because it is confusing to say and hear so many names at one time.

Suggestion: For practice, use your family group to pretend by saying, "This is my suite mate from college, Kathy Miller. She's visiting from Dallas." Then each member in the family may introduce himself or herself in turn at the appropriate time (using the six S's, of course)!

If a person . . . comes in while you're conversing, it's handsome to repeat what was said before.

George Washington

Just Passing Through

If you and a friend pass one of your other friends in a public setting, like a mall, it's not necessary to stop and introduce your two friends, because they will not be having a conversation. (If you do stop to visit, however, you should introduce them.) If the approaching friend doesn't stop, or if you don't wish to do so yourself—often because of time constraints— you may simply speak to each other in passing.

Suggestion: Go out in the yard, pretending you're at a mall or another public place, and let the kids walk or run by each other, not stopping to talk, but simply saying, "Hello, how are you?"

Be not froward but friendly and courteous,
the first to salute, hear, and answer.
George Washington

Part 3
Telephone Manners

You can tell more about a person by what he says about others than by what others say about him.
Leo Aikman

A Smile You Can Hear

Every time you answer any telephone, wear a smile! Your voice is all you have to communicate with over the phone. The person on the other end can hear the smile in your voice.

Suggestion: Let each family member look at another and say hello while frowning. Then look at the same person and say hello while you smile. (It's easier to frown after a smile than the other way around.)

For fun, place a small mirror near the family telephone and check yourself every time you answer it. You will be more aware of how you're responding to the caller—tired, irritable, lazy, disconnected, or uncaring. It also works when you make a call.

If we do meet again, why, we shall smile.
William Shakespeare

Who's This?

Even with caller ID (caller identification), always identify yourself when you call someone. Give your name as soon as someone on the other end of the line says hello. The recipient deserves to have you identify yourself. After all, a phone call intrudes on another person's time by default. Simply saying your name is the courteous thing to do.

Suggestion: Choose a family member as your partner, and call one another using a cell phone and a land line, if possible. Take turns calling and identifying yourself. One partner will say, "This is (state your name). May I speak to (the person you're calling for)?" Then let the other partner make the call and identify himself or herself.

It takes at least five attempts or practices to establish a habit.
Lois Gardner

Mumbo Jumbo

When talking on the phone, speak clearly. Don't mumble or garble your words. "Yeah" and "Who's this?" are never as good as "Yes" and "Who may I ask is calling?" An answer spoken at breakneck speed or in lazy jargon can be hard to understand.

For example, have you ever called a place of business and heard "Blah, blah, blah," as though the answerer was competing in a speed race? You probably had no idea if you had actually reached your intended telephone number.

Suggestion: Choose another family member and two telephones. Take turns identifying yourselves by speaking slowly and clearly. Give one another a gentle critique and continue practicing until you give the information in an understandable way.

The two new millennium mantras of the cell phone:
"I'm losing you" and "Can you hear me now?"
June Hines Moore

Open All Night?

When placing a phone call, always consider the time of day (or night). The generally accepted rule says, "Don't call anyone at home after 9:00 p.m. or before 7:00 a.m. unless the call is expected or unless the call is to report an emergency." No one wants to awaken to a ringing telephone to learn that someone has called for a trivial chat.

Suggestion: We are too easily addicted to convenience—fast food, remote controls, e-mail, on-line shopping, pills for our moods, cell phones. So among your family members, talk about the rules at your house for the time of day calls should and should not be made or received.

* * * * * * *

Life be not so short but that there is always time for courtesy.
Ralph Waldo Emerson

Wrong Number

When you make a telephone call and reach a wrong number, you should never simply hang up. No one likes to be hung up on, even when someone calls a number in error. The recipient of the call deserves an explanation. Always say you are sorry, and that you must have dialed the wrong number.

Suggestion: Discuss experiences each of you has had when you rushed to answer the phone only to hear silence, then a loud click, and then the dial tone. Talk about how that made you feel.

*Middle age: When you're sitting at home
on Saturday night, the telephone rings,
and you hope it isn't for you.*
Ogden Nash

Manners Saved My Life

Some of our etiquette rules are for safety. Therefore, it is necessary for everyone in the family to know how to punch in the number 911 on the phone in case of an emergency. Children who are not old enough to answer the phone and take a message can still practice finding 911 on the telephone.

Suggestion: Choose the best method for your family. One idea is to paint the 911 numbers with a dab of nail polish, and teach a child to start with the dot on the 9 and move up to 1, hitting it twice. (To practice this with your child, make doubly sure the phone is unplugged!)

*Recognize a problem before it
becomes an emergency.*
Arnold H. Glasgow

Dropped Calls

The individual who places the telephone call is the one who should say good-bye and hang up first, and if the telephone connection is broken, the caller should be the one to replace the call. If you both try to replace the call, you will hear only a busy signal. With a cell phone, it will usually go straight to voice mail. (In applying these rules, there is an exception: in business, the customer is expected to end the call or hang up first.)

Suggestion: Everyone in the family may want to practice being the one who makes the call and then the one who receives a call. You may gently critique one another.

The telephone, which interrupts the most serious conversations and cuts short the most weighty observations, has a romance of its own.

Virginia Woolf

A Crummy Connection

It is very bad manners to eat or drink while talking on the telephone. For one thing, sounds are magnified over the telephone, and it is very annoying to the listener to hear you eating and talking at the same time.

So if someone calls you while you are eating, ask if you may call them back. In fact, ask the person to name the best time for you to call so that you do not interrupt them while *they* are eating.

Suggestion: Choose a family member to practice with and experience the annoyance of listening to someone on the other end of the phone line crunching a mouthful of food, slurping a drink, or eating ice.

Manners are under our control.
Letitia Baldrige

One at a Time, Please

Do not talk on the phone while carrying on a conversation with someone in the room or in the car, because it is confusing to the person on the phone to hear you talking with others at the same time.

If at some point it becomes necessary to speak with the person in the room, excuse yourself for a minute from the phone call and return to the phone as quickly as possible, or ask the caller if you may return the call later. One conversation at a time is plenty for anyone.

Suggestion: To make this rule easier to remember, choose two family members to have separate conversations with, both at the same time. All three of you will have a difficult time keeping the conversations straight.

When your superiors talk to anybody, hearken not, neither speak nor laugh.
George Washington

Home Alone?

If you answer the phone and the caller asks for a family member who is not at home, it's not necessary to tell the caller that you are home alone. The reason for this rule is safety and privacy. Simply say, "I'm sorry, but he (or she) is not available. May I take a message?"

Suggestion: Practice what your family should say to unidentified or unknown callers, especially when a family member is home alone. For example, a young child should *never* tell a caller he or she is home without a parent or other adult. The child may simply say, "My dad (or mom) is not available." The child can ask the caller if he or she would like to speak to the baby sitter. That way the caller knows the child is not alone.

Caution is preferable to rash bravery.
William Shakespeare

Truth in Telephoning

Good manners and telling the truth go hand in hand. It is wrong to tell a lie on the phone by saying to a caller, "My dad can't come to the phone because he is in the shower," when in fact Dad simply doesn't want to talk to the caller. Telling the truth is the ninth of the Ten Commandments (found in the 20th chapter of Exodus). And, yes, it even applies to telephone manners.

Suggestion: For family practice, simply say, "He (or she) can't come to the phone right now. May I take a message?" There is no need to be more specific than that. Modeling by example is the best way to instill good manners.

"Beauty is truth, truth beauty"—that is all ye know on earth, and all ye need to know.

John Keats

Hey, It's for You!

When you answer the phone and the caller wants to speak to another family member, it is rude to yell out the person's name across the house, telling him or her to come to the phone. Unless you cover the mouthpiece, your loud voice becomes like a megaphone.

The time spent looking for the requested party (unless it drags on for several minutes) is never as annoying as the sound of your shouting coming through the phone line.

Suggestion: For family practice, pretend a call is for a parent or a sibling. Lay the telephone receiver down and quietly find the person whom the call is for.

Manners are very communicable:
men catch them from each other.
Ralph Waldo Emerson

After the Beep

Telephone message machines and voice mail can be wonderful conveniences, but there are rules to be followed in using these tools properly.

When recording your outgoing message, for example, be sure to speak slowly and clearly so the caller will know if he or she has reached the intended household. It is unsettling trying to decide if you should leave a message when the receiver doesn't announce the telephone number or leaves doubt that your message will be left at the right person's home.

Suggestion: Call home to check your outgoing message occasionally for accuracy and effectiveness. Electric power outages can erase your outgoing message, often without your knowing it.

Ceremonies are different in every country, but true politeness is everywhere the same.
Oliver Goldsmith

Who's Laughing Now?

The outgoing message from your phone should not be unnecessarily long, cute, or musical, because what may be "cute" to the owner of the phone can be very annoying and time-consuming to a caller. It's best to save your creative personality for times when you're actually at home and able to answer the phone, not when others are forced to endure it once again in order to leave you a message.

Suggestion: Talk about the recorded phone message with your family. Is it as short as possible? Does it give out the needed information? Try writing it out and reading it to the recorder. This way, your speaking is usually more efficient and includes fewer "uhs" and "ers." Your callers will appreciate it.

Keep your words soft and tender because tomorrow you may have to eat them.

Anonymous

Short and Sweet

A good outgoing message to leave on your telephone answering service is the following: "You have reached (your number). Please leave your message after the tone." You may give more information, if you like, but keep it short. For privacy concerns, it is not necessary to give the family name of the household.

One example of an outgoing message done in very poor taste was reported in the *Arkansas Democrat Gazette*: "Hi, I'm probably here. I'm just avoiding someone I don't like. Leave me a message, and if I don't call back, it's you."

Suggestion: You may choose to have a male record the message, especially if a female lives alone. Again, this is for safety reasons.

The use of telephone answering machines became popular in 1974.

Who Are You Calling For?

When leaving a message, it is proper to always speak distinctly and not ramble on for a long period of time. Give your name, your telephone number, and a brief message, including the name of the person you are trying to reach. It is also a good idea to state the time of day you are calling. The person who takes your message will need all of this information to know how to respond to you.

Suggestion: For family practice, let each member call the home telephone and leave his or her own message. Make sure each message covers the basics mentioned above in a clear, easy to understand manner. Gentle critiques may be helpful.

A fool may talk, but a wise man speaks.
Ben Jonson

Thank You Just the Same

It is not necessary to be rude when responding to unwanted phone callers (such as telemarketers, fund-raisers, and survey takers) because there are polite phrases you can use to quickly end the call and offend no one. Certainly, you will encounter some callers who are aggressive and unwilling to take no for an answer, but remember that no one can force impoliteness on you. Your response can still remain cordial, though firm and unwavering.

Suggestion: Discuss what to say when a tele-marketer calls. Be polite, of course, but be decisive. Say something such as, "I don't make such decisions over the phone," or "Thank you, but I am not inter-ested. Please put me on your 'no call' list."

Rudeness is the weak man's imitation of strength.
Eric Hoffer

Hurry Up and Wait

When you take a call for someone in your family who is not near the phone, do not ask callers to wait more than about twenty seconds without going back to see if they want to continue holding. The caller may prefer to call back later or leave a message. We should give him or her the choice.

Suggestion: Let each family member pretend to take a call for another family member, then register the amount of time spent waiting for that family member to come to the phone. Each member may be surprised how short twenty seconds is—but how long it seems when you're listening to silence.

Many a man wishes he were strong enough to tear a telephone book in half—especially if he has a teenage daughter.
Guy Lombardo

Call Waiting

You may find call-waiting a necessity. If so, there are some important rules. Good telephone etiquette requires that when you answer your call-waiting beep, the first caller takes priority because, as the old adage says, "First come, first served" (unless the second caller has an emergency or his call is otherwise extremely important). If you don't want to be interrupted, you can disable call-waiting, depending on your telephone service, before you place a call. This does not work with an incoming call.

Suggestion: Practice talking on the phone with a partner when a pretend beep comes in. Notice how annoying it can be when the one getting the beep leaves you "hanging on the line," so to speak. Let this happen to both partners and then discuss how it makes you feel.

There can be no defense like elaborate courtesy.
E. V. Lucas

Two for One

Another rule for the call-waiting beep is this: the one hearing the beep must ask the first caller if he or she can hold for you to answer the caller on the other line. Then—this is very important—*wait for an answer*, because the first caller may prefer to call back. It is good manners to respect the first caller's time.

Suggestion: Practice on the phone with a partner, asking if you may answer the call-waiting beep. Be prepared for a no answer. When that happens, be polite by saying, "I'm sorry, but I must take this call. I am expecting a call from the doctor." Remember how inconvenienced you felt the last time you called a friend and were repeatedly interrupted by call-waiting?

We use answering machines to screen calls, and then have call waiting so we won't miss a call.

Anonymous

Can I Call You Back?

If you do answer the call-waiting beep, it is important to tell the second caller about the first caller whom you have on the other line. The best approach is to ask the second caller if you may call him or her back after you finish the first call. Then say good-bye and return quickly to the first caller. Once again, respect the first caller's priority.

Suggestion: Practice with three family members and three phones, if possible. Respond to the beep by giving preference to the first caller, then asking the second if you can call back a little later. Keep working until you can do this without rudely interrupting the first caller or without appearing rattled by the intrusion.

* * ✦ * ✦ ✦ * ✦ * ✦

Sleep not when others speak . . . speak not when you should hold your peace.
George Washington

I Must Go Now

The primary exception to the previous manners entry is when the second caller—the one whose call activates the call-waiting beep—is phoning with an urgent message or is delivering information you must receive at that moment. When this happens, quickly go back to the first caller long enough to explain that you simply must take the second call, and that you will call the first caller back as soon as possible.

Suggestion: With two family partners, practice by asking the first caller to please excuse you because of an emergency. Again, keep working until you can do this quickly but without appearing curt and insensitive.

How much of human life is lost in waiting?
Ralph Waldo Emerson

Just to Let You Know

If you make a telephone call while already knowing that you may get an important call-waiting beep, it is polite to alert the person ahead of time. By telling the person in advance, you prepare them for an interruption if it happens to arrive later in the conversation. This is also true if you *receive* a call while expecting another important call.

Suggestion: Pretend to make a call, but alert the receiver of your call that you may be interrupted by your doctor or some other important call. Try to think of several examples of calls that rise to this level of urgency or importance.

Politeness is benevolence in small things.
Anonymous

Cell Phones

It is good manners to use discretion when using your cell phone. Make private conversations brief when you are in the presence of others. A cell phone can be a life-saving invention, but it can also be an annoyance. With over 80 million cell phones in use today, we should still remember that the people we are actually with, face to face, deserve our first attention unless there is an emergency.

Suggestion: Practice in the family by having individual cell phones ring during a family time together to see what an annoyance they can be. When a cell phone rings, you may choose to let the caller leave a message, or excuse yourself to take the call privately.

Cell phones are the latest invention in rudeness.
D. H. Mondfleur

Sorry, This Is Urgent

If expecting a potentially urgent call while at a performance or church service, put your cell phone on vibrate and sit as near the exit as possible. Your "emergency" shouldn't invade others' tranquil enjoyment. If you must take the call, talk in private.

This from the *Baltimore Sun*: "A single cell phone talker virtually seizes and occupies a public communal space and instantly converts it into his or her own. Anyone within earshot must listen to half a mundane or intimate fragment of a chat by and about matters and people of whom we know nothing and about whom we care less."

Suggestion: Talk about experiences when you were annoyed that other people answered their cell phones in your presence.

Being considerate of others will take your children further in life than any college degree.
Marian Wright Edelman

Would It Hurt This Once?

Even setting your cell phone on vibrate can be rude and disruptive, because the sound is usually still loud enough to attract attention and interrupt face-to-face conversation. Even if you choose to ignore it, others who are with you are not sure whether to mention it or not, to give you permission to see who it is.

Better, perhaps, when not expecting an urgent call, to learn to live the way we did in the "olden days"—before cell phones—when one of the chief blessings of being out with friends was not being interrupted by the telephone. Try turning the ringer totally off and see if you can live with it.

Suggestion: Make sure everyone in the family knows how to turn the cell phone off or to silence the ringer.

*Blessed are the merciful,
because they will be shown mercy.*
Matthew 5:7

Children and the Telephone

When children are about five or six, they can usually answer the telephone, taking and relaying an oral message. When children are able to write, they may take written messages.

A fun historical fact: Before telephones, "calling cards" were left with whoever answered the door. The owner of the card turned down the upper right-hand corner signifying a personal visit; the upper left corner, congratulations; the lower right corner, adieu; the lower left corner, condolence; the entire left end, a call on the whole family.

Suggestion: Practice with the younger children by calling from your cell phone to the household telephone, making sure they have pen and paper if they will be writing down your message.

In Atlanta, it's illegal to tie a giraffe to a telephone pole (during parades, I presume).

Guess Who Called?

When taking a message over the phone for someone, you should write down the information accurately and place it in a prominent place, where the intended recipient cannot miss it upon his or her return home. Messages that sometimes seem trivial to one family member may be very important to another. Do for them what you would like to have done for you when a call comes for you while you are away.

Suggestion: Pretend to be leaving a message on the telephone. Each family member can practice writing the message down, remembering to include the proper elements: name, number, time and date, and a short message.

The habit of being uniformly considerate toward others will bring increased happiness to you.

Grenville Kleiser

Message Board

Families should plan ahead of time to designate a central place where any phone messages (or messages of any kind) will be left. This way, whenever a person arrives home, he or she will know exactly where to look to see if any messages are present. Again, this is not only helpful for phone messages but also to alert other family members (if you have stepped out) where you have gone and when you expect to return.

Suggestion: Look for a certain spot in the house—perhaps somewhere in the kitchen, where everyone passes when they arrive home—so that you can identify one special place for messages. A cork board with stick pins, a bulletin board, chalkboard, or a magnet can be useful.

A man's manners are a mirror
in which he shows his portrait.
Johann Wolfgang von Goethe

Can You Hear Me Now?

One final summary statement about using the telephone: Always remember to speak clearly on the phone, knowing that callers are unable to talk with you face to face. The person on the other end cannot read your lips or see your facial expressions.

It takes a little more effort to emphasize your words and speak loudly enough to be understood. But everyone appreciates kind, considerate phone manners. And heaven knows we have a lot of opportunities to practice them, if we choose to.

Suggestion: As a family, discuss words that are difficult to understand on the telephone. Name those that should be eliminated or clarified, such as "whadaya want?" and "whoozis?"

It is good manners to prefer those to whom we speak before ourselves.
George Washington

Part 4
The Perfect Guest

*Etiquette means behaving yourself
a little better than is absolutely necessary.*
Will Cuppy

Mind Your Manners

An oft-invited guest must be well-mannered with a certain amount of self-control, as this story from Dr. James Dobson will attest: A college son brought his roommate, a football lineman, home for the weekend. The mom fixed a pound of bacon and a dozen eggs for breakfast. After the blessing, the dad picked up the platter holding the eggs and bacon and passed it to the guest. The young athlete moved his plate, placed the platter in front of himself, and then began to eat from it. The mom, though shocked, quickly began cooking more food for the family.

Suggestion: Think of a time when you could hardly wait for a guest to leave. Make a list of things that a welcomed guest should and should not do.

No guest is so welcome in a friend's house that he will not become a nuisance after three days.

Titus Maccius Plautus

Bring Enough for Yourself

For a sleepover, a guest should take along any toilet articles and other personal items (such as contact lens solution, toothpaste, shampoo, and the like). Do not put yourself in a position where it's necessary to borrow such essentials from the hosts. Make yourself as self-sufficient, unobtrusive, and inexpensive as possible.

Suggestion: Make a list of personal items each family member should always pack when going visiting. Having a personal checklist on the computer will make it easy to check off each time a family member packs his or her personal bag for a trip.

When you are invited by someone to a wedding banquet, don't recline at the best place.

Luke 14:8

Going My Way?

A guest should always be prepared to participate in whatever activities the host has planned. You are visiting in another person's home, and you are expected to flow along with the things they have planned for you—even those things they'd be doing whether you were there or not. When a guest is easily agreeable and cooperative, everyone has a lot more fun.

Suggestion: Talk about wording a polite request that you might make if the host or the invitation doesn't indicate what you should bring or wear. For example: "I'm not sure what you have planned for the weekend. May I ask if I should bring any special clothes or equipment?" (such as a tennis racket, swimsuit, or hiking boots).

What is more agreeable than one's home?
Marcus Tullius Cicero

Just a Little Something

An overnight guest should take a small, inexpensive gift to the host or hostess, unless the two friends are in the habit of exchanging overnight invitations regularly, such as a school friend or relative. A gift is simply a nice gesture to the host family, who may spend time and money to entertain you as a guest.

Suggestion: Talk about appropriate gifts for each member to take: a scented candle (vanilla or some other generic flavor) or a home-baked food item. You don't want to take something decorative that might not go well with the furnishings of the house or the hostess's tastes. The item must not be too personal either, such as bath powder or cologne. Compile a list of ideas on the computer.

It is more blessed to give than to receive.
Acts 20:35

Healthy Honesty

If you are a guest who has serious allergies or phobias, you should tell the host or hostess privately, ahead of time. The host family will not want you to suffer in silence or be embarrassed by not knowing you can't eat shrimp or are afraid of heights.

You're probably not alone. According to recent news reports, 12 million Americans have some kind of food allergies.

Suggestion: Name any allergies or phobias that might be a problem when you're away from home. It's important to remember that as a guest, you want to be as little trouble as possible. Simply having a dislike for spinach, however, is not a reason to expect your own private vegetable.

These fellow mortals, every one,
must be accepted as they are.
George Eliot

Can I Help You with That?

If you are eating as a guest where the family usually eats (not the formal dining room), you should offer to help clean up the dishes after the meal. Wait, though, until the hostess begins. You should offer only once or twice and not be a pest. Some hostesses prefer to do the chore alone or with another family member.

If you are a guest in someone's formal dining room for a very elegant meal, you should not offer. At formal dinners, guests do not go into the kitchen for any reason.

Suggestion: Choose a family member at each meal to be the guest who offers and helps clean up. Talk about your preferences when others are visiting with you: clean up with help or clean up alone?

He who eats with the grace of a garbage disposal is destined to a lonely life.

Anonymous

Hello to All

Upon arrival, a guest should say hello not only to the host or hostess, but also to any other family members present. As a visitor, you are the guest of the entire family, not just the friend who extended the invitation to you.

Suggestion: Pretend one family member is the guest, and let him or her greet the host (another family member) with a smile and a comment about how nice it is to be here, how he or she has looked forward to visiting. Then say something nice to others in the room, being sure to include everyone.

No stranger had to spend the night on the street, for I opened my door to the traveler.
Job 31:32

Manners Become You

A polite guest must obey the rules of the house. This can be a little awkward, but it is the respectful and appreciative thing to do. Just because the friend in whose home you're visiting is lazy and unhelpful to others in the family doesn't mean you have to be. Your good manners should still be on display.

Suggestion: Talk about chores you as a guest might help with, such as straightening up the guest room, making the bed, or helping clean up after dinner. Talk about what a difference it makes when a guest in your home readily and eagerly offers to help.

Noble be man, helpful and good! For that alone sets him apart from every other creature on earth.
Johann Wolfgang von Goethe

Something Old, Something New

It's not uncommon to feel a little out of place and uncomfortable in new surroundings, when you're not familiar with the habits and enjoyments of a different household. But if something they've planned for you to do with them is new to you, do it anyway. You might be pleasantly surprised and have some unexpected fun. You'll at least make a new memory!

Suggestion: Perhaps the parents or another family member might have a fun story about learning a new game or activity while visiting as a guest, or even about a time your family taught a guest something fun and new at your house.

She urged us . . . "Come and stay at my house."
And she persuaded us.
Acts 16:15

Rumbly Tummies

A child who is a guest in someone's home may ask for a snack if it's not too close to dinner or if the resident child has not already asked and been refused by a parent. An adult may do this, too, if there is a dietary or medical reason.

The hosts do not want a guest to be uncomfortable, and they have no way of knowing a guest might be hungry unless they are told.

Suggestion: Decide on acceptable ways to ask for something to eat. For instance, simply go to the host or the adult in charge and say, "May I please have a little something to eat to hold me until dinner?" Then gratefully accept whatever is offered.

* * * * * * *

A hungry stomach cannot hear.
Jean de La Fontaine

Ring of Shame

Never place a glass or anything that might leave an ugly mark or blemish on a piece of furniture. Use a coaster, a small mat, or a plate. The same goes for any surface or countertop that's not granite or meant to hold hot objects. If in doubt about whether your drink will leave a mark, be sure to err on the side of protection.

Suggestion: Talk about surfaces in your own home that require a coaster or hot pad. Notice any marks that have found their way onto the furniture from past carelessness. Make sure everyone knows where the coasters are kept, or have a fun shopping outing to go looking for some.

The greater the man, the greater the courtesy.
Alfred, Lord Tennyson

No Food Critics

At meals, a guest should try everything without commenting about the taste—except to say the food is good! To make a face or negative comment will hurt the host's feelings, especially if he or she went to a lot of trouble to prepare it. Saying, "I hate broccoli" will offend the cook.

Suggestion: Practice taking a very small bite and washing it down with milk or some other beverage. There is no etiquette rule that says we have to clean our plates. But by trying new foods, a guest may find he or she likes something after all.

So they gave a dinner for Him there.
John 12:2

Oops

A guest should treat the possessions of the family with respect and care. If the guest does have an accident with something, he or she should tell the host, apologize, and offer to clean up or replace the item broken or damaged, even if the host says it's not necessary. If the parent wants to do the cleaning alone, abide by those wishes. The soiled or damaged item may require special treatment. The guest should offer to replace a broken or damaged item, but don't belabor the issue.

Suggestion: Discuss how you would feel if your friend came to your house and destroyed your new game, even unintentionally.

Labour to keep alive in your breast that little celestial fire called conscience.
George Washington

All Together Now

To be a well-remembered guest, you should always be neat and keep your things together, not scattered from room to room or table to bed.

For example, carry your toiletries with you to the bathroom. Before you leave the bathroom, pick up your towel, rinse the sink, flush the toilet, and return your personal things to your suitcase. Don't leave them spread out in disarray over the bathroom counter or floor.

Suggestion: Talk about the above suggestions, and perhaps add to the list. Talk about how easy it is to lose or leave behind items if you're not careful about keeping them together. Compile your list on the computer or have someone do it for you.

*Don't think only about your own affairs,
but be interested in others, too.*

Philippians 2:4 (NLT)

Picking Up the Pieces

A guest should pick up his or her dirty clothes and keep them with his or her other things. No one wants to pick up after a guest, and no one wants to stumble over someone else's mess.

Suggestion: Decide which kind of household plastic or paper bags you might take in your suitcase to put your soiled clothes in on your next visit. (A few small holes in the disposable bag will help prevent mold and odor on wet clothing or shoes.) A paper grocery bag, neatly folded, or a small, clean, plastic garbage bag will usually work well. The size of the bag should be determined by the length of the visit.

Your manners are always under examination by committees little suspected . . . awarding or denying you very high prizes when you least think of it.
Ralph Waldo Emerson

Hold Your Fire

A guest should wait his or her turn to talk, because interrupting others is rude and unpleasant, even though the host's family members are not likely to scold.

As the Bible says, "If anyone thinks he is religious, without controlling his tongue but deceiving his heart, his religion is useless" (James 1:26).

Suggestion: Discuss how being interrupted makes you feel. Talk about ways to politely enter a conversation with phrases such as, "Please excuse me" or "May I tell you about my experience?" when there is a break in the conversation. Also, talk about the value of not talking when others are engaged in an intense or serious discussion.

There cannot be greater rudeness than to interrupt another in the current of his discourse.

John Locke

Making the Bed

A guest should make his or her bed daily, even if the hostess says doing so is not necessary. When the visit has concluded, the guest should ask the hostess about taking off the sheets and putting them in the laundry. If the guest is told to remove the sheets, he or she should do so and put the bed covering back in place. A well-remembered guest will always leave things clean and tidy.

Suggestion: Make sure everyone in the family knows how to make a bed. For instance, start with the cover sheet, straightening it by pulling it toward the pillows. Next, bring the covering up, smoothing out any ripples. You may not do a fantastic job, but do your best.

I am thankful for the piles of laundry and ironing because it means my loved ones are nearby.
Nancie J. Carmody

One and Done?

A guest should be prepared to use his or her bath towel more than once, hanging it up after each use. Some families make this their custom. It cuts down on laundry chores.

Suggestion: Talk about some of the unspoken customs your family operates under, like perhaps using a bath towel more than one time. Then talk about what to do if you are unsure about a matter like this when you're visiting, such as getting a fresh towel when you're not offered one. You may always ask your hosts what they would like you to do.

Don't reserve your best behavior for special occasions. . . . You must be the same to all people.
Lillian Watson

No Peeking

A guest should always respect the privacy of others by not eavesdropping or snooping around. You as a host would not want your guest sneaking around or opening drawers and cabinet doors in your house. Remember the Golden Rule: "Do unto others as you would have them do unto you."

Suggestion: Make a list of things you as a guest should not do while in another's home, such as opening a closed door without knocking; entering a room uninvited where two people appear to be having a private conversation; snooping in drawers, closets, or cupboards.

A peace above all earthly dignities,
a still and quiet conscience.
William Shakespeare

Excuse Me

If a guest needs something urgently, has a personal difficulty, or must enter a room or interrupt briefly, he or she should ask. The host may not otherwise realize the guest needs something, and most hosts want to provide for the needs of their guests.

Suggestion: Talk about some of the reasons you might need to ask your host for something and how you should do so. For instance, simply say, "Excuse me, please. May I get my glove to go to ball practice now?" Upon leaving the room, of course, be sure to say, "Thank you."

Become useful and helpful and kind to one another, tenderhearted (compassionate, understanding, loving-hearted), forgiving one another readily and freely, as God in Christ forgave you.
Ephesians 4:32 (AMP)

Phone Home?

A guest should not make telephone calls without asking permission. Telephones in private homes are personal possessions of the family, and outgoing calls home may be long-distance and expensive.

Suggestion: Talk about what to do if you are visiting and need to call home. For instance, if your call is long distance, you may use a credit card or make arrangements with your family for the call before you leave home and reverse the charges. If you use someone's cell phone, be sure to ask about his remaining minutes for the month or whatever his plan states. Always offer to pay.

*In my walks it seems to me that
the grace of God is in courtesy.*
Hilaire Belloc

Who Pays?

A guest should expect to pay his or her own way unless the host family insists on paying the expenses for a planned activity, such as a restaurant meal or some other outing or event. Never just assume that your host will be picking up the bill.

Suggestion: Talk about how to offer to pay for a movie ticket, for instance. Offer once with money in your hand by saying, "I'll get mine," or something similar. But don't insist or make a scene about it. Don't protest one way or the other. Neither the host nor the guest should be embarrassed over financial arrangements.

Etiquette is what you are doing and saying when people are looking and listening. What you are thinking is your business. Thinking is not etiquette.
Virginia Hudson

Pick Up, Clean Up

A guest should always help clean up and put games or equipment away. If you want to be someone who is invited back and enjoyed as a guest, be sure to do your part with household chores and other acts of helpfulness and cooperation.

Suggestion: Talk about how each member can help when he or she is the guest at someone else's house. When play is finished, for instance, don't simply offer but begin picking up the pieces of the activity to return them to the box. After a meal, offer to help with the dishes. The hostess may not want or expect your help, but she will be glad you thought to ask.

Many hands make light work.
John Heywood

Everybody to Bed

A sleep-over guest should abide by the "going to bed" and "getting up" rules of the house, because other people who live there may have a heavy schedule and need their rest. Even if their bedtime schedule is not what you're accustomed to, you shouldn't disturb others by either staying up too late or sleeping in, causing others to be inconvenienced around you.

Suggestion: Share experiences you have had while trying to sleep when someone's noise disturbed you. Talk about being an early riser or a night owl and how a guest should be quiet while others might be sleeping or resting.

In courtesy I'd have her chiefly learn,
hearts are not had as a gift but hearts are earned.
William Butler Yeats

Before We Go Any Further

When a child is visiting in another's home and it comes time to leave, he or she should ask the friend (and then a parent) if there is anything that needs cleaning up or putting away. It is a thoughtful guest who wants to leave everything in order before departing, not carelessly skipping out as though it's the host's job to pick up after him.

Suggestion: Talk about or make a list of things that a guest should help with before leaving. Talk about times when you've had to go to great lengths to pick up after a guest who left without helping to tidy things.

Manners are the happy ways of doing things.
Ralph Waldo Emerson

Packing List

A guest should carry a list in his or her suitcase of everything packed for the visit so the host family doesn't find it necessary to return items later. Remember, it is your own responsibility to take care of your personal belongings, and being doubly sure what you packed is a good way to help you do that.

Suggestion: Try putting individual lists of family members' belongings on the computer for easy accessibility when packing for a visit. When it comes time to leave, simply print the list off and put it in your suitcase. You can check the list as you pack for the visit and again when you pack to return home.

The word responsibility has three "I"s in it.
Anonymous

Leaving So Soon?

Upon leaving a person's home—whether you particularly enjoyed yourself or not—a guest should always be sure to thank the host or hosts for inviting him or her. It makes a host feel good when a guest says he or she had a good time. It is the gracious thing for the guest to do.

Suggestion: Practice what each of you might say to a host upon departure, even if you're really glad to be leaving and going home. You may say as much as you like, but be sure to say, "Thank you for inviting me." And if you had a genuinely good time, say so.

Everyone who exalts himself will be humbled, but the one who humbles himself will be exalted.

Luke 18:14

Bread and Butter

If you're an overnight or out-of-town guest, write a thank-you note as soon as possible after you get home—even if you thanked the hosts personally before leaving. This is called a bread and butter note. It is a gracious and long-standing tradition.

Suggestion: To help your family practice composing these so-called "bread and butter notes" after an overnight visit, acquire notepaper and matching envelopes for every family member. If you don't have your own note cards, use a nice piece of paper and an envelope. It is not necessary to write a long letter, but you should write it by hand, not on the computer. Simply say something nice about your visit, perhaps the food or the activities.

For the person who knows to do good and doesn't do it, it is a sin.
James 4:17

Part 5
The Gracious Host

What is pleasanter than the tie of host and guest?
Aeschylus

Returning the Favor

After we have been someone's guest, we should return the favor and reciprocate the invitation in a similar fashion, perhaps as a dinner guest or a weekend guest. It is not necessary, however, to duplicate the hospitality of one's host exactly. Instead of entertaining in your home, you may take your friends to a nice restaurant.

Suggestion: Talk about what it means to entertain someone in a similar fashion and to reciprocate an invitation. Name an occasion when your family has hosted someone who later invited all of you over for a fun time. Perhaps your family invited someone to dinner at your house, and later that guest invited you to a meal at their church.

It is not the quantity of the meat, but the cheerfulness of the guests, which makes the feast.
Edward Hyde

Clear Invitations

A gracious host communicates the details of the invitation clearly so that the guest will not be embarrassed by arriving late, bringing the wrong clothes, or staying past the expected time of departure.

Suggestion: Make a list of things you should write or tell a guest when you invite him or her. For instance, say, "We would like you to come at 7:00 for dinner on Friday evening, then my parents will be happy to take you home Saturday afternoon" or say, "See if your parents can pick you up around 5:00 on Sunday afternoon."

Go out into the highways and lanes and make them come in, so that my house may be filled.

Luke 14:23

Thinking Ahead

A gracious host should anticipate the needs of the guest ahead of time, in order to make him or her more comfortable and happy while visiting in the home.

Suggestion: Plan a weekend invitation to a friend or a family. Then make a list of chores, naming the family members who will take care of each one in preparation for the company. For instance, everyone will want to clean his or her room and make space for the friend's belongings. One member may want to purchase tickets to an event so that the family and guests do not have to stand in line. Another member may want to prepare a special dessert.

Behave to everyone as if you were
receiving a great guest.
Confuscius

House Rules

To prepare well for an expected guest, consider the kinds of things that might be unique about your home or manner of living that would need to be mentioned up front. Think about the routine things he or she will be needing and how your guest can locate them in the house. Show the guest how to turn on the shower or to lock the bathroom door, if they are troublesome.

Suggestion: Let each family member put himself or herself in the guest's place. Pretend they're entering the front door as a guest and don't know where things are in the house. Let another member make sure the guest is shown where the bath linens are kept or where to hang his or her clothes.

Hospitality is making your guests feel at home, even if you wish they were.
Anonymous

Hats and Coats

To make a guest feel welcome, a gracious host always offers to take a guest's hat, coat, or suitcase at the door, showing the guest where he or she will be able to find them when they are needed. A guest likes to have instructions about what to do and when to do it to avoid embarrassment.

Suggestion: Assign one family member the role of guest and another the role of host. The host member takes the guest's suitcase and puts it in a secure, accessible place where it will not mar the furniture. He or she hangs the guest's clothes in the closet.

He welcomed us courteously and
fed us for three days.
Acts 28:7

Names and Faces

When the guest arrives, a gracious host should show the friend around the house and introduce him or her to other members of the family who may be present so the guest will feel more comfortable. When guests meet and talk to other members of the family, they feel less like an outsider and more at home.

Suggestion: It could be fun to practice by assigning members to the guest's and host's roles. Show the guest where the bathroom is and where the bedroom is where he or she will sleep. Talk about other things to show the guest.

It is a sin against hospitality to open your doors and darken your countenance.

Anonymous

Something to Eat?

Unless it's mealtime or you're immediately leaving to go out to eat, a gracious host always offers guests a snack or refreshment upon or soon after their arrival. Food and beverages represent warmth and comfort to us. Sharing food is like sharing a part of us. It sets people at ease and makes them feel good.

Suggestion: Talk about beverages or snacks you might offer a guest, such as water, diet soda, regular soda, tea, or coffee. Also, talk about things that are inappropriate to offer, such as leftovers from last night's dinner.

It is a true saying that a man must eat a peck of salt with his friend before he knows him.
Miguel de Cervantes

What Do You Like?

A gracious host should plan activities around the likes of his or her guests by asking about the guest's preferences ahead of time. You want to know what will make your guest the most comfortable and the least likely to be embarrassed or to feel pressured.

Suggestion: Let family members tell about what a good time they had at someone's house because the host asked them about their likes and dislikes. If you learn, for instance, that your guest is afraid of heights, you will not likely plan a trip to the tallest building in town. Or if your guest cannot swim, you may decide to stay away from water.

The nearer you come into relation with a person, the more necessary do tact and courtesy become.
Oliver Wendell Holmes

Stick with Me

A host is responsible for attending the needs of the guests, which means staying available while the friend is a guest in the home. Guests may be unsure what to do if left alone.

Suggestion: Share experiences about being left alone or feeling out of place while visiting a friend. This discussion will remind others to be alert when there is a guest in the house, even if the guest was invited by another family member. Also, discuss not turning your guests over to another family member to entertain while you go off on your on.

What do we live for, if it is not to make life less difficult for each other?
George Eliot

All in the Family

All family members should be hospitable to any guests in the house. If you are the brother or sister of the inviter, be courteous and engage in some polite conversation to put the guest at ease. It is very uncomfortable to feel that one family member appears unhappy you're there or is unfriendly toward you.

Suggestion: While keeping cool heads and remembering the Golden Rule, talk about how it feels to have a guest in your own house when others in your family are not nice to him or her. Name some things you can do individually to help.

♦ ♦ ♦ ♦ ♦ ♦ ♦

A word is dead when it is said, some say.
I say it just begins to live that day.
Emily Dickinson

Guests Go First

A gracious host always lets the guest be first in any activities. When it comes time to play a game, let the guest not only choose what to play but also be the first to choose his or her playing piece.

Speaking of putting your guest first, here are some ways to really spoil them: 1) An arrangement of flowers to fill the room with scent and color. 2) A basket of snacks and bottled water. 3) Books or a journal by their bedside. 4) If there is electronic equipment for entertainment, leave the remote controls easy to find.

Suggestion: Invite a neighbor or other friend over to play a game, and put this "gracious host" rule into practice.

Love each other with genuine affection,
and take delight in honoring each other.
Romans 12:10

Not Here, Not Now

The well-mannered host never asks another family member something embarrassing while a guest is in the home. For instance, if you're not sure whether or not a parent would want you do something, don't put your parent on the spot to defend his or her reasons in public. Or if something less than flattering about another family member comes to mind in conversation, keep the memory or comment to yourself.

Suggestion: Talk about your family's plan for such situations, such as excusing yourself for a moment from your guest while you go find a parent, then ask quietly if you and your friend may play with the family karaoke machine.

Discretion is the better part of valor.
William Shakespeare

Let's Talk Later

A gracious host should not talk on the telephone to a friend for an extended time, leaving his or her guests to entertain themselves. Your guests will feel ill at ease and lonely, as though you might prefer it if they weren't there.

Suggestion: Talk about your families' rules for talking on the phone while guests are present. For instance, if a friend calls while you have a guest, explain to the caller that you have company and cannot talk long on the phone. (The caller would want the same courtesy shown to him or her if the situation were reversed.)

Make your guests feel welcome and at home. If you do that honestly, the rest takes care of itself.
Barbara Hall

Ready to Go?

A proper host should help any guest find his or her belongings when it is time to pack up and leave. Being less familiar with the household, the guest might not readily remember where all his or her things are. Make your final words and actions be remembered as gracious even after the visit is over.

Suggestion: Talk about helping guests pack up and get ready to go home. For instance, when it comes time for guests to leave, ask if you can help pack, but don't insist. However, even if the guests say, "No, thanks," it's a good idea to stay close by in case you are needed after all.

It is wise to apply the oil of refined politeness to the mechanisms of friendship.

Colette

Part 6
Church Manners

Everything must be done decently and in order.
1 Corinthians 14:40

Get Me to the Church on Time

Everyone should be on time and enter the church with a respectful attitude, observing the dignity of the place and the people. Arriving late disturbs the worshipers who did arrive on time.

A recent newspaper article outlined some of the ways decorum has left our church services. Some congregants sip from water bottles or fast-food cups, read newspapers, pop their gum, stick it under the seat of the pew, and fail to remove bawling babies from the sanctuary. Arriving late and leaving early could be included in this list.

Suggestion: Getting started the night before can help get you to services on time. Go ahead and choose the clothes everyone will wear. Polish shoes, iron hair ribbons, gather Bible materials and so forth the night before.

Punctuality is the politeness of kings.
Louis XVIII

What to Expect

If you are invited to an unfamiliar church, it is proper to inquire about the dress, the customs, and perhaps the rituals you may need to know in order to show respect and avoid any embarrassment.

In Omaha, for example, it is illegal to burp or sneeze in church. Missouri statutes say it's unlawful to play hopscotch on the sidewalk on Sunday. But seriously, finding out about the church you're attending will help you know how to prepare and what to expect when you get there.

Suggestion: Before the day, Mom or Dad may ask questions of the family or minister who invited them. There may be a nursery for your very young children. Inquire about the ages for whom child care is provided and what you are expected to bring.

♦ ♦ ♦ ♦ ♦ ♦ ♦

*Let our advance worrying become
advance planning and thinking.*
Winston Churchill

Kindly Remove Your Caps

Men and boys should remove their hats as a sign of respect before entering a Christian church. In some churches, the women respectfully wear a hat or veil over their heads.

Dress matters in the way you approach worship. I like the way one article stated it: "Jeans don't belong at the symphony, baseball caps and shorts at theatrical events, bare midriffs in the workplace, or strapless sundresses or miniskirts in church." I wholeheartedly agree.

Suggestion: Explain to your children why Dad removes his hat before entering the church building. Talk about other dress expectations that go along with worship and church attendance.

Holiness becometh thine house, O Lord, for ever.
Psalm 93:5 (KJV)

The Golden Rule

The Golden Rule takes precedence over any other rule of manners or social graces. It is also the universal rule: "Do unto others as you would have them do unto you." The major religions in the world all have a version similar to our Golden Rule. Mankind seems to naturally understand the truth of God conveyed through this simple guide to relationships and interaction.

Suggestion: Talk about the universal meaning of the Golden Rule and how it should help us make decisions about the right things to do. Be sure this is one that everyone in your family has memorized (Luke 6:31).

One of the troubles in the world today is that we have allowed The Golden Rule to become a bit tarnished.

Martin Vanbee

Other Customs

In synagogues, men and boys wear yarmulkes, and females have their arms and shoulders covered. If you and your sons are visiting but are not Jewish and do not have yarmulkes, each of you will likely be given one to wear as you enter the synagogue.

Suggestion: It is a good idea for families to know something about other religions after they are thoroughly grounded in their own beliefs. To be well-mannered, we must respect the beliefs and religion of others even if we don't subscribe to them. Parents can set an example by following rules and traditions of whatever house of worship they enter.

To love Him with all your heart, with all your understanding, and with all your strength, and to love your neighbor as yourself, is far more important than all the burnt offerings and sacrifices.
Mark 12:33

Wait Till Later

Do not chew gum, unwrap noisy candy wrappers, or talk on your cell phone in a church service or a wedding because the noise will disturb others. Since we're accustomed to having what we want—when we want it—it's tempting to seek this kind of instant gratification in church, as well. Learn the self-discipline and self-control of respecting the church service.

Suggestion: If you have young children who must have a snack, go prepared with something edible that is noiseless, such as breath mints. Even a senior official in the Turkish government was recently charged with insulting the country's founding leader by chewing gum during a ceremony. How much more disrespectful this is to the Lord himself.

It is not desirable to cultivate a respect for the law, so much as for the right.
Henry David Thoreau

Children's Church

Proper manners allow young children to quietly write or draw in church, but not on the visitor cards or flyers, because doing so is wasteful and disrespectful.

Incidentally, here's one "Sunday" fact that will interest your children: The sale of ice cream was once banned on Sundays in Ohio because it was deemed frivolous and luxurious. Merchants, therefore, began topping the ice cream with scoops of fruit, thereby deeming the dish healthy and nutritious. Lo and behold, the "ice cream sundae" was invented.

Suggestion: Unless doing so violates your family's rules, take pencil and paper or markers with you for your children to use whether you are going to your own church or someone else's.

Let the little children come to Me. Don't stop them, for the kingdom of God belongs to such as these.
Mark 10:14

Communion

Holy Communion is observed in most churches and in a variety of ways, because each religious organization has its own rituals, sacraments, observances, and customs. (Communion is usually some form of bread and drink, which the congregants partake of together.)

Suggestion: In some churches, only local church members take communion. In others, those who take Communion go to the altar at the front of the church. If you're visiting in a church like this, you may remain quietly and reverently at your seat unless the minister invites everyone to the altar. It is never rude to respectfully ask questions about the church's customs before you attend.

This is My blood that establishes the covenant; it is shed for many for the forgiveness of sins.
Matthew 26:28

No Running

Children shouldn't run or push in a church building, not only for safety reasons but primarily out of respect. It is up to parents (as well as teachers) to help children develop a healthy sense of respect for the place of worship, realizing that what happens inside as people interact with God is not to be taken lightly.

Suggestion: Parents might want to talk to their children before reaching the church. Without scolding, a parent can be positive and say, "I know you will remember your church manners when we get there and not run or push. We will all need to be reverent." (It's much more difficult to instruct after you are inside.)

You are to conduct yourselves in reverence during this time of temporary residence.
1 Peter 1:17

Seating Procedures

If ushers are not in sight when you reach the church, Dad should lead the way to the family's seats. If there *is* an usher, Mom should follow the usher as her family follows her with Dad in the rear.

There is a general rule of safety etiquette that says a man should lead any time there is no one else to lead the way in public and when there is an element of danger or the unknown.

Suggestion: Talk about how your family will enter the church before you reach the door. If there is no usher and Dad leads the way down the aisle, he stands aside for his wife and children to enter the pew, then he follows them. You might even decide to practice at home.

*Whatever curiosity the order of things
has awakened in our minds, the order
of things can satisfy.*
Ralph Waldo Emerson

Bathroom Breaks

Participants in a church service should not go in and out—going to the bathroom, for instance—but should remain in their place throughout the service unless they go to the altar or must leave to take out an unruly child. Reverence and respect demand both of these rules. Care must be made in all ways to avoid distracting others or to draw your own attention away from worship.

Suggestion: Discuss how you can remind one another to make sure everyone in the family makes a trip to the bathroom and the water fountain if necessary before going into the sanctuary for worship.

So that you may be devoted to the Lord without distraction.
1 Corinthians 7:35

If You're Late

If you arrive late and the church service has already begun, do not enter during a prayer or a musical presentation. Doing so is rude and disrespectful to everyone. Wait if possible until all the congregants are standing so that your presence will not be as noticeable.

Suggestion: Discuss as a family how you plan to wait at the back of the church until there is a break in the service, perhaps as people are being reseated after the singing of a hymn. Let this also be a chance to talk about the importance of arriving on time to begin with, making these other arrangements unnecessary.

*God is greatly feared in the council
of the holy ones, more awe-inspiring than
all who surround Him.*
Psalm 89:7

The Act of Worship

Adults and children alike should stand and take part in the church service as much as they are able, according to their age, maturity, and comfort level. The word "worship," after all, is a verb. It implies action and alertness. Worship is something we are called to participate in, not merely watch and spectate—and certainly not to ignore or tune out of.

Suggestion: If your church utilizes hymnals, hold the book so that the person standing next to you can read from it also. For a young child, you can follow the words and the music with your finger. If you or your child sings out of tune, no one will mind.

Serve the Lord with gladness;
come before Him with joyful songs.
Psalm 100:2

Keep It Down

Adults and children are expected to be reasonably quiet in any church service in order to provide a worshipful atmosphere for everyone. Some customs and styles of worship encourage participants to be more vocal than others, but avoid drawing attention to yourself or anything that interferes with another person's experience with God.

Suggestion: If you have a young child, you may want to sit near an exit if you suspect he or she might need to leave. Some churches have a "crying room." If your child cries loudly and uncontrollably, you should remove the child from the service.

An inability to stay quiet is one of the conspicuous failings of mankind.
Walter Bagehot

Nice to See You

Members of almost any religious congregation should greet guests and visitors in order to make them feel welcome and comfortable. Although some church services have a welcoming time when members stand and greet the people they do not know, it's still a good idea to look for someone after the service to greet and introduce yourself to.

Suggestion: If your family members are attending as guests or prospective members and no one introduces themselves to you, try introducing yourself and your family to an usher or an elder at the entrance or to someone near you in the pew.

Treat everyone with politeness, even those who are rude to you—not because they are nice, but because you are.

Anonymous

Agree to Disagree

It is important to show respect for the beliefs of others by not criticizing or making fun of them. At the same time, make sure your children know what you believe and hold dear. Each one of us wants others to respect our system of beliefs and practices.

Suggestion: Children mimic their parents. Family members should be role models for one another. So in your times of discussion together—or even in your informal conversations—be sure your comments about others are made with respect, and your differences of opinion are truth-based and not personal.

*Whenever you feel like criticizing any one,
just remember that all the people in this world
haven't had the advantages that you've had.*
F. Scott Fitzgerald

Funerals

Taking a child to a funeral is a decision for the parents to make, not a set rule of etiquette. However, the age, maturity, and demeanor of the child should be considered before making the decision to attend because of those who may be grieving. Put their needs above your own in this matter.

Suggestion: If you decide to take your children to a funeral, explain to them what to expect. The service may be a memorial with no casket, or the funeral may be in a funeral home, or the service may simply be beside the grave. This is also a good opportunity to talk about the value of life, being grateful for others, and the importance of putting one's trust in God, who has victory over death.

O Death, where is your victory?
O Death, where is your sting?
1 Corinthians 15:55

Receiving Visitors

When attending the "family visitation" time before a funeral, friends should be quiet, dignified, and attentive to the grieving family. Visitors should not have private conversations on topics unrelated to the deceased and the family. Children should be as quiet and unobtrusive as possible, even though their vitality and warmth can be quite healing in such sorrowful settings.

Suggestion: Teach your children ahead of time never to run, talk loudly, or meddle while you are visiting the family of the bereaved. Know where your child is at all times. Explain how your family would feel if you lost a loved one.

Manners are a sensitive awareness of the feelings of others. If you have that awareness, you have good manners.
Emily Post

Funeral Dress

Etiquette no longer mandates that only black may be worn to funerals, because some families choose to celebrate the life of their loved one. However, casually-dressed funeral-goers should not call attention to themselves. The service is not for or about them but the family of the deceased.

Suggestion: If you are to be seated with the family at a funeral, or if you are a pallbearer or usher, try wearing black or a dark, subdued color. To respect local customs, ask someone ahead of time if you are in doubt about what to wear.

They say such nice things about people at their funerals, it makes me sad to realize I'm going to miss mine by just a few days.

Garrison Keillor

Other Kinds of Customs

A Jewish funeral takes place within the shortest time possible after a death, because Jews believe that the soul has returned to God and that it is shameful to have the person's body remain with the living.

Suggestion: Using this reason, explain to your children that there will be no embalming and no open casket where you can "view the body" in this kind of situation. Additionally, the Jewish custom is to wash your hands when leaving a cemetery. You may do this as you leave or just before you enter the home of the bereaved. (See also MyJewishLearning. com.)

Blessed are those who mourn,
because they will be comforted.
Matthew 5:4

Forward Looking

Churchgoers should face the front at all times unless told to look behind them for some reason. It makes others uncomfortable to have someone turn around and stare at them.

Manners, you see, are always appropriate. At dinner one evening, a little boy named Josh bowed his head, folded his hands, asked the blessing, and let out a big burp. Looking up and seeing his dad's look of disapproval, he put his head back down and prayed, "Excuse me, Jesus."

Suggestion: Remind your children before entering the church not to turn around in the pew. During the service, try gently turning them forward when they forget.

When you speak of God or His attributes,
let it be seriously and with reverence.
George Washington

Thanks All Around

It is good manners to show respect and appreciation to church teachers and workers, especially if they work with your children. These dedicated individuals offer themselves freely to minister and show God's love to our families, and they deserve regular expressions of thanks, more than just words of thanks said in passing.

Suggestion: As a parent, show your gratitude for the time and efforts of all the church teachers. Offer to help the teacher any way you can, just as you would do in school. Write them a note during the year or at the end of the church year.

Now we ask you, brothers, to give recognition to those who labor among you.
1 Thessalonians 5:12

Part 7
Electronic Etiquette

*I push and push on the foot pedal
and nothing happens!*

Computer help-line caller (in obvious need of mouse skills)

Online Considerations

New technology demands new etiquette rules to learn because in 1922, when Emily Post wrote her first etiquette book, she never imagined computers and the Internet. Yet it remains a rule of etiquette to respect others' time and sensibilities—even online. Consider the impact a message might have before hitting the "send" button.

Suggestion: Talk about using rules of courtesy when going on the Internet, being kind with words and clear in their writing. Check your messages for the following: Is the message clear? Is the wording kind? Are correct grammar and spelling used? Have I written a positive and informative message? What about sarcasm and jokes? Both can be easily misunderstood in cyberspace.

Kindness is a language the deaf can hear and the blind can see. It's the same in any language.

Anonymous

Netiquette

The word "netiquette" is a combination of the words *net* and *etiquette*. Together they describe the rules for using the Internet. Rules of etiquette are required to make communications in cyberspace pleasant, civilized, and efficient.

Suggestion: Share among family members any tips learned about good netiquette in school or at work, such as being careful with acronyms like BTW for "by the way." Your reader may or may not understand, so these should only be used for very casual messages. One that is good to use is NRN even in business, which means "no reply necessary." Your readers will like that one.

A lie gets halfway around the world before the truth has a chance to get its pants on.

Winston Churchill

Onboard Editor

Send only e-mail messages that you would put on a postcard or handwritten letter for anyone to see, because cyberspace is very public. With the right technological skills, someone can find and read your message. Our e-mails are not as private as we may think they are.

Suggestion: Discuss the lack of privacy for your messages on the Internet and what it means to send a message on a postcard. Imagine stumbling upon words said about you by someone who never would have wanted you reading them.

For all its speed and convenience,
there is something intrinsically shallow
and superficial about e-mail.
Cox News Service

Chain Letters

Never send and pass along e-mail chain letters, because they are legally forbidden. A violation can actually get your network privileges revoked. These chain letters—messages sent simultaneously to hundreds of people—usually promise rewards if you send the message to your friends, family members, and others to keep the chain going.

Suggestion: Talk about the need to alert a parent or other family member if and when you receive a chain that's been forwarded to you. Discuss the telltale signs of chain letters—music, clip art, angel stories, petition drives, cultural scares—to help one another spot them at a glance.

Chain letters are the postal equivalent of intestinal flu: you get it and pass it along to your friends.
Bob Garfield

Keep Your Voice Down

Never write messages with all letters capitalized, all letters in lowercase, or in a bold font or typeface. To emphasize a single word or phrase, you can enclose it in asterisks or write it in italics. Messages written in all uppercase, lowercase, or in bold letters are very difficult to read. Also, always use spell check before you hit the "send" button.

Suggestion: Talk about experiences you may have had when receiving a message written in all caps or in all lower case letters and why doing so is a bad idea. Both are very difficult to read.

Do not use all capitals in e-mail exchanges.
It is considered SHOUTING and is rude.
The National Courtesy Council

May I Address You?

Never give out someone's e-mail address without his or her specific permission. You can lose a friend that way, or worse, get into trouble with the law. A person's e-mail address is one's own private property, and he or she should always be in control of how it is disseminated or distributed.

Suggestion: Let family members tell of any experiences they may have had with someone giving out their e-mail address and why it is a bad idea. Your family may decide to have a family rule about such things.

Compaq® is considering changing the command "Press Any Key" to "Press Return Key" because of the flood of calls asking where the "Any" key is.
Wall Street Journal

Spam on the Menu

Do not send, forward, or reply to spam mail. It wastes time and space in an inbox, not to mention placing people's computers at danger of being corrupted by malicious viruses and other problems.

The term "spamming" describes any unwanted, irrelevant messages, usually sent to large, unsolicited mailing lists, often selling unsavory products and containing crude language or images.

Suggestion: Look up the word Spam®, and you will find that it's the name of a canned meat product that is a hodgepodge of many different meats. On the Internet, spam can be a hodgepodge of extra, wasted verbiage or advertisement. Talk about what makes spam such a problem and how you can avoid it.

It has become appallingly obvious that our technology has exceeded our humanity.
Albert Einstein

Long-Winded Letters

If your personal communication on an e-mail is going to be lengthy, include the word "long" somewhere in the subject header of the e-mail or in the opening line of your message. (A message of over one hundred lines, by the way, is considered long.)

Just make sure the recipient knows to expect a prolonged correspondence, so that he or she can delay reading it till a later time if preferred.

Suggestion: Talk about sending messages as attachments if they are very long, so that they can be more easily printed out or dealt with. Knowledge-able family members can perhaps teach the others how to do this if they don't know.

Blessed is the man, who having nothing to say,
abstains from giving wordy evidence of the fact.
George Eliot

Reply to All?

Do not send unsolicited mail to people whose names you happen to see on a mailing list. Just because you are included among a long list of other recipients to an e-mail message does not give you permission to correspond with them all if they're not expecting you to. This invades another's domain without their consent, and it is rude. Make your response only to the sender of the e-mail.

Suggestion: Talk about how annoying it can be to find a large number of unwanted e-mails that you must consider before determining which ones to delete and which to answer.

*A people that values its privileges
above its principles soon loses both.*
Dwight D. Eisenhower

Inbox or Mailbox?

E-mail and the Internet are not the appropriate venues for all communication. Some messages, even in our current technological age, must still be hand-written to convey their most effective sentiments. Personal notes and letters have a special power and purpose all their own.

Suggestion: Talk about these messages: a note of congratulations, a hospitality note, a thank-you note, a letter of apology, a letter of introduction, and a condolence or sympathy note. Name others you can think of which should be handwritten.

E-mail is disposable, but handwritten letters and notes can be cherished for years.
Anonymous

Be Safe Out There

Some etiquette rules apply to all Internet users because such rules protect our family members from encountering harmful images or activity online. Children, for example, should never give out their address or telephone number on the Internet without a parent's permission. Never download an attachment if you do not know and approve the source. Never agree to meet another person you have met on the Internet.

Suggestion: Discuss the above with all family members. Make sure everyone is clear on what is acceptable online behavior—and what is not. For your entire family's safety, these decisions need to be made ahead of time.

Do not be deceived:
"Bad company corrupts good morals."
1 Corinthians 15:33

Fax to Consider

A fax (facsimile document) is transmitted by a facsimile machine and should be considered public information by both sender and receiver. It travels over the phone lines to another fax machine that prints it out for anyone to see. Therefore, the sender should call ahead to alert the receiver of the incoming fax.

Suggestion: Speedy communication on a fax machine may be less expensive and more efficient than a telephone call. But talk about why you should not send anything of a private nature by fax, and remember to respect the time and resources of the recipient of your fax.

The more elaborate our means of communication, the less we communicate.
Joseph Priestly

Covering All Your Bases

The rules say to include the following with every fax you send: a cover sheet with the date, the name of the sender, the sender's fax number and telephone number, the name and fax number of the recipient, the page count (including the cover sheet), and a brief message or explanation of the faxed material to come on the pages transmitted.

Because faxes are written and not spoken, there is no two-way communication; therefore, all the information on the cover sheet is necessary.

Suggestion: Talk about reasons why junk faxes are never welcome, such as a waste of time, paper, and ink.

*Make everything as simple as possible,
but not simpler.*
Albert Einstein

Forward Thinking

It is rude to forward a lot of e-mail messages, photos, and "cute" things without permission. What may be funny and indispensable to you could just be a waste of time for someone else. Better to tell someone in person about a funny or otherwise enjoyable message you received, then let him or her ask if you would forward it along.

You should also get permission from your friends before sending links to Web sites.

Suggestion: Talk about unwanted messages in one's inbox and about inboxes filling up unnecessarily. Establish a family rule about sending forwards and keeping the inbox cleaned out. Some families have reported how excess mail has jammed their computers.

Well-timed silence hath more
eloquence than speech.
Martin Fraquhar Tupper

The Better to See You With

For any e-mail messages that you do decide to forward, be sure to delete all the imbedded e-mail addresses to previous recipients that may still appear in the e-mail trail. To do this, you must hit "forward" first, clean up your message, then hit "send." This not only protects the addresses of other people, but also keeps your recipient from having to navigate around them in order to locate the message.

Suggestion: Talk about your experiences with troublesome e-mails. Share any remedies you have discovered. Discuss, too, your family rules for dealing with incoming forwards—whether to delete them immediately or to get a parent's permission before opening them.

*I quote others only in order
the better to express myself.*
Michel de Montaigne

Being Cute Doesn't Cut It

It is not good etiquette to use obscure symbols called "emoticons" in serious e-mail correspondence. They are fine, of course, in casual messages to personal friends and other informal communications. It's important that we know the difference between the two.

Suggestion: Discuss the emoticons and e-mail text abbreviations you know. As a family, see who knows the meanings of these emoticons and acronyms, such as :-) :(BTW, LOL, FYI. List some of the others you know. As mentioned before, NRN (which means "no reply needed") is one of the few abbreviations that is appropriate for professional correspondence.

The art of art, the glory of expression and the sunshine of the light of letters, is simplicity.
Walt Whitman

Blind Carbon Copy

If you are sending a group e-mail to a large mailing list of otherwise unrelated individuals, address the message to yourself, and then "blind carbon copy" (bcc) everyone else. That way, your friends' addresses will be kept private. When you use bcc, each recipient of your message will see only their name and yours.

By the way, if your children don't know the origins of what "carboning" means, tell them about the blue carbon paper that was once used to make duplicates of documents on a typewriter.

Suggestion: Go to the family computer and practice sending e-mails to your family using the information above.

The true measure of a man is how he treats someone who can do him absolutely no good.
Samuel Johnson

Multi-Layer Messages

It is bad manners to send messages with more than one "forward." Sometimes you get a message that contains a forwarded message which, when opened, contains another forwarded message. This might require you to click through five or six layers before you get to the message.

One way to block such messages is to set your spam filters to block messages with more than one "FW" in the subject line.

Suggestion: Let family members practice copying and pasting the body of a message into an e-mail to prevent sending too many messages with too many "forwards."

Good manners is the art of making those people easy with whom we converse.
Jonathan Swift

Part 8
The Words We Say

I don't care how much a man talks,
if he only says it in a few words.
Josh Billings

Tongue in Cheek

Coping with manners of the tongue is one of the biggest challenges families face. We all use our mouths to get what we want, express our hearts, and make our opinions known. As parents, we do well to use good mouth manners and a friendly tone in dealing with other members of our family. Children do well when they use good mouth manners with parents and siblings.

Suggestion: See how long you can go without using scolding or angry words. You may want to make a chart to post on the refrigerator or family message board.

To disagree, one doesn't have to be disagreeable.
Barry Goldwater

Hello, How Are You?

Family members should greet and politely respond to friends and acquaintances of their parents and siblings, because that is the way they would like their own friends to be treated. Not to speak to another person, even out of shyness, gives the appearance of rudeness.

Suggestion: Greet a friend of your parents with "Hello, Mrs. Peters." When Mrs. Peters says, "Hello, Melissa, how are you?" Melissa should say, "I am fine, thank you," or give a similar response. The best response is "I am fine, Mrs. Peters, thank you." Repeating Mrs. Peter's name is very nice.

A grunt is never acceptable. Hello is nice.
Erma Bombeck

Please and Thank You

The words "please," "thank you," and similar words work like a boomerang. When we use these words, they usually come back to us. People who habitually say "please" and "thank you" are nice to be around and often have many friends.

Suggestion: Let each family member keep score and see who can use "please" and "thank you" the most. Say, "Please, pass the salt to me, Kevin" and "Thank you" after you receive it. Or learn together how to say "thank you" in another language, such as the French, "Merci."

British English provides a special word—"ta"—to serve as both "please" and "thank you," which is taught just as children begin to talk.

Sorry about That

Etiquette rules encourage us to say "I'm sorry" when we make a mistake, hurt someone (with words or actions), or bump into someone. Sometimes we do these things unintentionally.

The best expression of regret is "I'm sorry," not "It wasn't my fault" or "I didn't mean to do it." Saying "I'm sorry" means taking responsibility for our actions and showing genuine concern. You should be more interested in another person's harm than your own innocence.

Suggestion: Keep score to see who can remember to say "I'm sorry" the most. Discuss saying the words "I'm sorry" and sounding like you mean it, not in a sarcastic slur.

Never ruin an apology with an excuse.
Kimberly Johnson

Excuse Me

It is proper to say "excuse me" or "pardon me" every time you think you might be offending or inconveniencing someone. Saying "please, excuse me" or "please, pardon me" usually creates good will and eases tempers. Asking someone to excuse us or pardon us is a minor inconvenience or confession that shows we care, that we're aware of the other person's needs, that we're noticing him.

Suggestion: Try counting the times in an hour when you can find a good reason to say "please, excuse me" or "please, pardon me" for some infraction, blunder, mistake, or mishap.

Even steel loses its strength when it loses it temper.
Anonymous

Yes and No

It is proper in the South to respond to adults' questions by answering with "yes, ma'am" and "no, sir." In other parts of the country, parents more often teach their children to simply say "yes" or "no" when responding to a question or request. Either of these methods teaches a child to show respect, while "yeah," "yo," and "uh-huh" are lazy expressions and are never appropriate.

Suggestion: Try saying "yes" or "yes ma'am" and other variations of these polite answers in your family. If you do, these expressions will likely become a habit to be proud of.

*Let your word "yes" be "yes,"
and your "no" be "no."*
Matthew 5:37

That's Nice of You

When someone says something nice about you, accept it graciously and say "thank you" or "It's kind of you to notice." Saying, "Oh, this old thing?" or "I should have done it better" is often our way of fishing for more compliments to be said.

Compliments, by the way, are kind comments about something a person is responsible for doing, such as listening or cooperating. Flattery is excessive, insincere praise, often meant to embarrass the one being complimented.

Suggestion: Try complimenting other family members about things they do well. When you receive a compliment, always say "thank you." See who can come up with the most sincere compliments to give another.

Nothing is so great an example of bad manners as flattery.
Jonathan Swift

The Truth in Love

Telling the truth is a virtue all family members should strive to achieve. Learning the difference between lying, telling the truth, and using tact is very important, because telling the truth pleases God and is the ninth of God's Ten Commandments. Truth said tactfully should not hurt someone.

Suggestion: Family members can be brutally honest sometimes. Talk about being kind even when the truth is not pleasant. For example, when a family member receives a present that he or she doesn't want or even like, learn to say, "Thank you for giving it to me," or "Thank you for taking time to shop for me" instead of saying, "I hate it."

Your conscience teaches your mind how to think, your heart to feel, and your soul to obey.
Anonymous

Ouch, That Hurts

Scripture tells us to treat others as we want to be treated, because words and actions can often hurt others' feelings. Also, when we hurt others' feelings, we won't have as many friends, and we will likely suffer the same ill treatment from our peers.

Suggestion: Discuss being kind, not hurtful. For instance, when you see a person with a disability, do not blurt out, "Why is your hand crippled? or "Why does your little brother walk like that?" Talk about how badly it makes people feel when someone makes fun of them. Instead, say something like: "Can I help open that door for you?"

Feelings are much like waves;
we can't stop them from coming,
but we can choose which ones to surf.
Lasse Mårtensson

Is That the Truth?

One serious mouth problem is lying. And we all have so many opportunities to practice it—and to try avoiding it! That's why getting in the habit of truth-telling is so important, because telling one lie often only succeeds in bringing out another one.

Suggestion: Talk about being truthful without telling everything you know, telling only what is necessary. For instance, if a family member lies by saying, "Tell her I'm not at home" when someone comes to the door, this sets a bad example for others. Instead of saying, "He's not here" (when the whole truth is, "He doesn't want to talk to you right now"), say, "I'm sorry, he isn't available right now. May I take a message?"

Be not apt to relate news if you know not the truth thereof.
George Washington

That's Not Funny

Do not laugh at another's bad jokes or racial slurs. Simply look the other way or ignore the person. Without an audience, the talker soon tires of trying to be funny at someone else's expense. In some cases, you can speak up and object in order to defend the one being disparaged or verbally abused.

Suggestion: Talk about times when you have seen or heard people talk badly about others. Discuss how to behave in those circumstances. Parents can evaluate that conduct and teach a better way if the young student is on the wrong track.

Coarse and foolish talking or crude joking are not suitable, but rather giving thanks.
Ephesians 5:4

Cutting In

Interrupting others who are talking is very rude. A person interrupts by asking questions or making remarks while another person is speaking, disregarding both the speaker and the normal flow of conversation. Interrupting a person who is talking is offensive to everyone present. Better to wait your turn and never get your point made than to trample on others.

Suggestion: Let family members talk about how it feels when other family members interrupt. Keep score to see who can go the longest time without interrupting anyone else in the family. Discover what a difference it makes when everyone is not talking all at once.

The mind is refrigerated by interruption.
Samuel Johnson

Pardon the Interruption

Occasionally there are times when interruptions are necessary, such as when an urgent phone call comes in for another family member, or when Mom is entertaining friends and your little brother is in danger of falling out of a tree.

Suggestion: Decide on a hand signal or some other physical way of showing that an interruption is absolutely necessary. The family member with the urgent interruption can simply say, "Please excuse me," or he or she can make eye contact or raise a hand to get another's attention. Establish in your family what constitutes an emergency and, on the other hand, when the interrupter should simply wait for the attention of the other family member.

Courage is what it takes to stand up and speak; courage is also what it takes to sit down and listen.
Winston Churchill

Contradiction in Terms

Contradicting others is very rude. (To contradict means to express an opposite opinion or to deny another's statement.) The speaker has the right to express an opinion—just as much as anyone else. Contradicting can be the same as calling someone a liar, though that is seldom our intention.

Contradictions usually come as interruptions when we blurt out our opposite point of view, thereby doubling the offense. Sometimes it is necessary to disagree with someone, of course, but it is never acceptable to be rude and unkind.

Suggestion: Decide as a family on some alternative phraseology to use, such as "Are you sure…?" or "I didn't understand it that way."

Do not condemn the judgment of another because it differs from your own. You may both be wrong.
Dandemis

Quiet Down

Unless there is a fire or someone is dying, it is almost never appropriate to yell out. Yelling startles people. To make things worse, tempers sometimes flare in response to yelling.

Suggestion: Yelling for a sibling whom Mom wants to come downstairs is a big temptation that can be overcome. Also, as mentioned before, make it a rule that whoever answers the phone must find the person who is needed rather than yelling out for him or her. Keep score to see who can remain calm and not yell for the longest period of time (hopefully for days).

A whisper can be stronger, as an atom is stronger, than a whole mountain.
Louise Nevelson

Watch Your Language

Swearing includes the use of any foul or vulgar language, especially using the Lord's name (God, Jesus, and Christ) in ways that are flippantly casual. Swearing breaks the third of God's Ten Commandments. It also shows a lack of self-control on the part of the swearer. Some say that it reflects the swearer's limited vocabulary.

Suggestion: Discuss the fact that family members will hear God's name used in an irreverent, profane way all their life, but they do not have to join the swearers. Modeling good language before others will reap great rewards. As a family, you may decide to tell people that God and Jesus Christ are special friends of yours and that you are offended when those names are used derogatorily.

*The Lord will not let you go unpunished
if you misuse his name.*
Exodus 20:7 (NLT)

Accentuate the Positive

It is impolite and even hurtful to make fun of the way someone speaks, such as with a different accent. We learn our speech patterns from our family. Criticizing or making fun is an insult to others and their heritage. They may, in fact, think *we're* the ones who talk funny.

Suggestion: Get involved with people of different cultures, accents, and customs. While remaining patriotic, family members can learn to accept other cultures. Join an "English As a Second Language" organization and teach someone to speak English. "It is not good to show partiality," the Bible says (Prov. 28:21). Rather, we are to affirm, accept, and appreciate others.

God loves each of us as if there were only one of us.
Augustine

Good Job

One way for families to consistently practice good "mouth manners" is by praising and recognizing one another's achievements. Genuine, deserved praise will reinforce positive, constructive behavior, while all the while creating more harmony within the household.

Suggestion: Be specific in saying good things about an accomplishment of another family member, such as, "I liked the way you laid out your clothes last night for school today." Don't say, "Well, it's about time you laid out your clothes. I've told you often enough." You might say to a sibling, "I'm happy for you that you caught that fly ball in the game tonight."

*Sandwich every bit of criticism between
two thick layers of praise.*
Mary Kay Ash

It Gets You Nowhere

Flattery is a form of bad manners. Flattery is an unearned compliment perceived as being nothing but false praise. It almost always comes across as insincere—praising someone for something he or she has no control over.

Suggestion: Discuss the difference between a flattering remark and a genuine compliment. While saying "You're a good boy," is not bad, try saying, "I noticed that you held your tongue when the boy broke in line." To build the self-respect that comes from the Lord, practice praising a specific accomplishment, something the person actually did.

I hate careless flattery, the kind that exhausts you in your effort to believe it.
Wilson Mizner

A Good Joke

Some people think good manners and a sense of humor don't go together. Not so! Developing a good sense of humor and a taste for what's funny makes you an enjoyable friend.

But there is never a place for dirty, inappropriate humor. It should always be clean and should not get laughs at another's expense. Good humor takes some of the edge out of an otherwise dreary day.

Suggestion: At the dinner table or in the family car, ask everyone to tell a funny story. Perhaps they heard it on the radio or read it in a book. Maybe it happened at school today or came from something a teacher told during class. Stipulate that all jokes must be good clean fun that doesn't hurt anyone's feelings.

Everything is funny as long as it is happening to somebody else.
Will Rogers

Just Between Us

It is bad manners to correct another's grammar or remarks unless it is welcomed, done politely, and said in private. Sometimes corrections are necessary and, yes, it is kinder to correct than to remain silent. But there is a right way to do it.

Suggestion: Start with the word "I" instead of "you" when expressing a difference of opinion. For instance, you can tactfully say, "I thought the teacher said Chapter 12 until I saw the assignment on the board saying we are to study Chapter 13." Correcting information this way is kinder than saying, "You got it all wrong." Let each family member practice giving their corrections in a polite, kindly manner.

In one generation we have gone from "I'm sorry" to "What's your problem?"
Anonymous

Say Something Nice

Having good manners means never saying un-kind things to or about one another. This includes things like gossiping and mocking others. As hard as it can be to do, drive these tendencies and habits from your life before you get yourself into trouble and hurt other people.

Suggestion: Discuss handling a situation when others use bad speaking manners. One approach is not to participate in the name calling or gossiping. Be silent and don't laugh at someone else's expense. Silence is sometimes the best way to quiet the one who is speaking critically or negatively of another. Another approach is to make a positive comment about the person being bad-mouthed.

A gossip goes around revealing a secret,
but the trustworthy keeps a confidence.
Proverbs 11:13

Sticks and Stones

"Sticks and stones can break my bones, but words can never hurt me." This is an old saying we've all heard before, but the truth is far different. Words can and often do hurt. In fact, it is often difficult to forget unkind remarks. The pain lingers. Think about it the next time you're tempted to offend another person.

Suggestion: Use an activity such as watching a clean but funny family show on television or DVD. Point out occasions when an unkind remark may be meant to be funny but is instead hurtful. Let each member of your family recall a time when words were hurtful to him or to her.

May the words of my mouth and the meditation of my heart be acceptable to You, Lord, my rock and my Redeemer.
Psalm 19:14

Part 9
Public Manners
and Traveling

The hardest job kids face today is learning good manners without seeing any.
Fred Astaire

Thanks for the Lift

When riding in someone else's car, you should behave as a guest—parents and children alike—just as if you were in someone's home. Riders should always be appreciative when riding with someone because riding in another's car is usually a courtesy and a privilege.

Suggestion: Talk about what it means to be well-mannered in someone's car—things like keeping your feet off the upholstery and not lowering or raising windows without permission. See how many of these you can name. Also, be sure to say "Thank you for the ride" when you get out of someone's car. You get extra points for using the driver's name. For instance, "Thank you for the ride, Mrs. Evans."

Courtesies of a small and trivial character are the ones which strike deepest in the heart.
Henry Clay

Rules of the Road

Anyone entering a car should greet everyone inside because being in the car with others makes for a close environment.

It is also important to sit where you are told to sit and to join in the conversation when you can. This shows respect for the driver. The seating arrangement in the car may even be for reasons unknown to you, such as allowing a passenger who tends to get carsick to sit near a window.

Suggestion: Practice greeting others (even in your own family) when you enter a car or when someone gets into yours. Say, "Hi, Adam, how are you today?" Think of some positive subjects for conversation that are appropriate for car travel.

Be nice to people on your way up because you meet them on your way down.
Jimmy Durante

Fasten Your Seat Belts

All passengers in any car should wear a seat belt for safety. This should be an instant, unquestioned habit—the first thing you do upon entering the car. Never let this rule of safety slip into compromise and disuse. Passengers should feel not quite dressed without their seat belt.

Suggestion: Practice by seeing who can put his belt on fastest after everyone is in the car. The best way to teach others to wear their seat belt is to wear one yourself. The driver is responsible for seeing to it that everyone is buckled up before the car moves (except for adults who may have a phobia about being restrained in a car). Within your family, you may want to devise some minor penalty.

*Fear is the father of courage
and the mother of safety.*
Henry H. Tweedy

Grab Your Stuff

Passengers should be responsible when entering and leaving someone's car. It's best not to take a lot of things with you in the car that are unnecessary. But remember to remove all the belongings you did bring when you get out. Items left in someone's car become clutter and a burden to the owner.

Suggestion: Practice being in a car with several things in your hands. When you get up to leave, make sure you remember all your belongings. Also, name as many points as you can about leaving any car, such as thanking the driver, telling the others goodbye, and closing the door gently but completely.

So didst thou travel on life's common way,
in cheerful godliness.
William Wordsworth

Look Both Ways

When exiting a car, always walk in front of the car so the driver can see you. Also be sure to watch for other vehicles coming in either direction. This etiquette rule, like many others, is based on safety.

Suggestion: Talk about the dangers associated with exiting and walking around a car or any moving vehicle. Why is it less dangerous to cross at the front of a car than the back? What are some other hazards to be watching for? Establish and practice a plan for automobile safety so that each member of your family can execute it.

Road sense is the offspring of courtesy and the parent of safety.
Australian traffic rule

Display Pieces

Always mind your manners in public so that no one will think you have bad manners. Our manners are things that are always on display when we're away from home or with others—always making an impression, either a good one or a bad one.

Suggestion: Talk about the difference between "showing off" to be noticed and being remembered as polite and courteous. Discuss how your family views this, comparing your values to those who think we should have little to no regard for what others think about us.

Things do not pass for what they are, but for what they seem. Most things are judged by their jackets.
Baltasar Gracián

Looking Good

Grooming is an affair to be done in private. We should never clip our nails; comb our hair; pick our teeth, nose, or ears; spit; wipe our mouth or nose on a sleeve; blow our nose without a tissue; and never apply makeup in public, especially at the table. Doing such things disgusts others.

Suggestion: Name some other inappropriate personal activities. Perhaps family members can tell stories of inappropriate behavior they have observed in public. (Caveat: It is bad manners to laugh at people we know or at those who don't know any better.)

Good manners sometimes means simply putting up with other people's bad manners.
H. Jackson Brown, Jr.

A Fitting Appearance

By age five (or about the time they start school), children become more socially aware and should be able to understand that what they wear is important. Their dress and grooming habits present an impression—not just of them but also of the family.

Suggestion: Talk about how the way a person looks shows respect or disrespect for the people he or she is with. Let family members recall ways that people choose the appropriate attire for their sport or for the beauty contest they want to enter.

Clothes and manners do not make the man,
but, when he is made, they greatly
improve his appearance.
Henry Ward Beecher

Nothing to Sneeze At

Sneezes should always be covered. When they're not, hordes of germs can be scattered onto bystanders if the sneeze is not caught in a tissue or the hands.

Suggestion: Talk about ways to handle an unexpected sneeze, such as handkerchiefs and tissues. Older family members can show the younger ones how to turn their head and sneeze into their sleeve or other clothing (if no tissue is handy) so they won't spread germs to others. Also, talk about washing one's hands as soon as possible after a sneeze.

If you cough, sneeze, sigh, or yawn,
do it not loud but privately, and speak not
in your yawning, but put your handkerchief
or hand before your face and turn aside.
George Washington

Sneezing Fits

When you feel a bout of sneezing coming on, you should excuse yourself and retreat from the group. A "bout" would be defined as continually sneezing or coughing—anything that is truly disturbing or annoying to those who feel captive to it.

Suggestion: Talk about what action to take if you find yourself in a public place—such as church, a meeting, or the movies—and you can't seem to stop coughing. The best choice, of course, is to quietly say "excuse me" and slip out of the room.

In Nebraska, it is illegal to sneeze in public.

Bless You

It is proper but not necessary to say "bless you" or "gesundheit" when someone sneezes. This comes from an old superstition that said a sneeze could cause the soul to fly out of the body unless someone blessed the sneezer. This isn't true, of course, but the practice of saying "bless you" is still a kind way of reacting sympathetically.

Suggestion: Talk about how your family feels about superstitions. It is generally considered appropriate to say the traditional "bless you"—unless this goes against your family values! If someone says it after *you* sneeze, it's important to say "thank you." Practice both, as your family chooses.

Gesundheit *is German for "good health."*

Cover Up

When you feel a sneeze or a cough coming on, you should turn your head down and to one side, covering your mouth with whatever you can—even your napkin, if that is all you have. By turning your head down and to one side, you will be sure not to sneeze on your food or on your neighbor.

Suggestion: Using a handkerchief, practice sneezing and coughing as politely and discreetly as possible. (Children love pretending this, but don't let them become offensive in doing so.) After sneezing or coughing, be sure to say "excuse me" or "pardon me" to those nearby.

Love and a cough cannot be hid.
George Herbert

Burp

When you must expel air from your mouth (belch), you should always cover your mouth. Burping is a common human frailty—perhaps a necessity at times—but it can also be disgusting to others. Suppress it as best you can, silently, and make a quick apology if you cannot.

Suggestion: Talk about ways to handle a sudden gas attack. For instance, always keep your mouth closed. If a burp is unavoidable, cover your mouth with your hand and say "pardon me." Talk about how impolite it is to talk or laugh about the problem, whether it is yours or someone else's.

Belch near no man's face with a corrupt fumosity.
Turn from such occasion; it is a stinking ventosity.
The Boke of Nurture (The Book of Nature)

Mind Your P's and Q's

There is an expression about practicing proper etiquette in public called "minding our p's and q's." The meaning of this expression comes from long ago when typesetters practiced their craft using their hands, placing metal letters individually onto the printing press to form words. They were very careful when choosing the letters p or q because the distinction between the letters was only in the way they were turned.

Suggestion: Talk about how minding our manners compares to choosing a p or q in writing.

May my meditation be pleasing to Him;
I will rejoice in the Lord.
Psalm 104:34

Name Tags

According to the National Institute of Business Management, a name tag should be worn on the right shoulder. This is because, as you extend your right hand for a handshake, the person you are greeting can easily see your name as their eyes travel from the handshake up your arm to your name tag. Decorative and ornamental pins are worn on the left.

Suggestion: Talk about ways to remember your name tag placement, and also about never criticizing someone who has his or hers pinned on the left. Remember never to embarrass someone (even a family member).

There is an emanation from the heart in genuine hospitality, which cannot be described but is immediately felt, and puts the stranger at once at his ease.
Washington Irving

When Nature Calls

A necessary part of life, of course, is going to the bathroom. So there are polite rules that guide us in public. For instance, no one wants to be reminded of what happens in the bathroom. It is seldom, if ever, necessary to announce, "I have to go to the bathroom," because even hearing that is offensive.

Suggestion: Family members can simply say "excuse me a moment" and exit. If a teacher is present, a child can quietly raise his hand or whisper to the teacher the reason for being excused. Talk about how things that may not be offensive to one person may, in fact, be offensive to others. Discuss being sensitive to everyone's feelings, never being crude or bringing up matters that are private in nature.

Love one another. Just as I have loved you, you must also love one another.
John 13:34

Wash Your Hands

Washing one's hands before leaving a restroom is not only good manners, it is obligatory. The obvious reason for doing so is to prevent the spreading of germs.

Suggestion: Be a good role model in your family by washing your hands. Remind one another to use a paper towel or tissue to open the door to a public bathroom when you exit. People before you may not have washed their hands, leaving germs on the door handle. Be sure to throw the paper towel or tissue in the proper receptacle.

We should wash ourselves clean from every impurity of the flesh and spirit, making our sanctification complete in the fear of God.
2 Corinthians 7:1

Bathroom Germs

Proper behavior in any bathroom demands that we flush the toilet and properly discard any used paper towels or tissue. With good manners in our heart, we should desire to leave the bathroom facility clean and neat for the next person.

Suggestion: Take the younger children to a public bathroom, instructing and demonstrating to them the proper use of public facilities. You may want to establish a family rule about an adult or older child accompanying a younger one to a public restroom. At the right age, talk about predators who sometimes lurk in public places.

According to an outdated statute, having a bathtub in your house in the state of Virginia is forbidden. It must be kept in the yard.

Bad Breath

Bad breath is offensive, and it is a worthwhile effort to take precautions against it—using breath fresheners, brushing your teeth often, avoiding certain spicy foods in certain situations. But it is also rude to embarrass people by telling them in front of others that they have halitosis. They may be unaware.

Suggestion: Discuss what to do if someone's bad breath is disturbing you, such as simply backing a step or two away to avoid the odor. If the person with the offensive breath is a close friend or relative, you may discreetly slip a breath mint into his or her hand with no comment.

Eat no onions nor garlic,
for we are to utter sweet breath.
William Shakespeare

Excuse Me

An honest "excuse me" can grease the friction of human interaction like a car bumper that keeps us from colliding.

Suggestion: Practice using the words "excuse me," even when the offense is made by someone else. For instance, say "excuse me" when another person bumps into you, even if the offender apologizes. Going out of your way to be polite when you are not obligated to do so improves your image and makes life sweeter. Talk about the dignity of taking responsibility for your actions whether anyone notices or not—even within your own family.

The essence of good manners consists in freely pardoning the shortcomings of others although nowhere falling short yourself.

Erasmus

Public Politeness

Public manners include the rules governing the use of elevators, escalators, stairs, revolving doors, and other doors. We comply with such rules because they keep us from embarrassing ourselves. The guiding principle in these situations, of course, is to let others go first, giving them preference in all things (one exception: revolving doors; see #216).

Suggestion: The next time you're using an elevator, try these rules: when getting on, always stand clear of the open doors and allow the passengers to get off before you try to enter. When approaching a door where others are coming in or out, give way to them before entering.

Good manners are made up of petty sacrifices.
Ralph Waldo Emerson

Elevator Logistics

In a crowded elevator, the individuals standing nearest the door get off first. Women and children always used to get off first, but that is not very practical when the elevator is crowded. When entering or exiting an elevator, you should make sure your belongings such as a hat or umbrella do not poke others or block their view, especially when someone is trying to exit.

Suggestion: Use a doorway in your home as an elevator door and practice coming through, emptying out in the proper order. Also try doing so while carrying packages or other items in your arms.

I would rather sit on a pumpkin and have it all to myself, than be crowded on a velvet cushion.
Henry David Thoreau

Uncrowded Day

When an elevator is not especially crowded, it is proper for ladies and any elderly persons to exit an elevator first because the males and younger passengers can easily move out of the way and hold the "open door" button. The gender rule applies here. In our society, we defer to ladies and the elderly. (To defer means to decide to let others go first.)

Suggestion: Pretend that only two or three of you are on an elevator. Then practice letting the ladies and the older members of your family exit first.

Nothing is ever lost by courtesy. It is the cheapest of the pleasures, costs nothing, and conveys much.
Erastus Wiman

Open Door Policy

The person closest to the "open door" button on an elevator should hold it until everyone enters or exits who needs to do so. Pressing this button will prevent the elevator doors from forcibly closing on someone.

In fact, especially if you're entering an elevator you're not accustomed to riding, it's not a bad idea to make a deliberate effort to locate the "open door" button as quickly as possible. If you wait until you need to push it, you'll have a hard time finding it.

Suggestion: The next time you're in a public elevator together, make sure each family member knows which button to push to keep an elevator door open so that others can enter.

Politeness and consideration for others is like investing pennies and getting dollars back.
Thomas Sowell

Push and Pull

The rules for opening doors differ for various kinds of doors. When entering pull doors, for example, always look behind you to see if someone is close by and could be let in before you, such as a person carrying an armful of packages.

When entering push doors, go ahead and pass through the doorway, then hold the door for anyone who may be approaching from the other side. It's difficult and awkward for others to squeeze between you and the doorframe.

Suggestion: Practice these rules in your house. Stress that these rules are not merely for etiquette's sake but are also designed for safety and efficiency.

*Courtesy, like grace and beauty, begets liking
and the inclination to love one another.*
Michel de Montaigne

Slamming Doors

Never let a door slam in someone's face. Besides being rude, this can be very harmful. Always look around you before entering or exiting through a doorway to see if anyone needs your assistance with the door.

Suggestion: Talk about the various reasons why someone might need your help entering or exiting a doorway. Think about times when you've needed the same kind of courtesy but found yourself having to fumble with the door handle all by yourself.

When one door closes, another door opens; but we so often look so long and so regretfully upon the closed door, we do not see the ones which open for us.
Alexander Graham Bell

Revolving Doors

Entering a revolving door has special rules for men and women because revolving doors are usually heavy and somewhat difficult to maneuver.

If the door is in motion, the gentleman stops the revolving door to allow the lady to enter first. Then he steps into the compartment in front of her and slowly moves the door. If the door is still as they approach, the man steps in first while she steps into the space behind him. Then he pushes it slowly.

Suggestion: Take the family to a building with a revolving door to practice. It takes a few tries to get a feel for how to do this.

Manners are more important than laws,
and upon them, to a great deal, the law depends.
George Bernard Shaw

Holding Patterns

It is still polite for men to stand ready to open doors for ladies. In earlier times, women wore long skirts and could not see the step down on a carriage. It became courteous practice for the man to hold the door while the lady descended.

Today, some doors are very heavy. Therefore, the practice of men holding the door for ladies is still a profitable politeness. Doors should also be held open for all guests coming into your home, as well as any doors *within* your home.

Suggestion: Practice being ready to open a door for another family member. Simply step carefully ahead of them and say, "Let me get that door for you."

The smallest act of kindness is worth more than the grandest intention.
Oscar Wilde

A Friendly Stroll

When a gentleman and a lady walk together, it is proper for the man to walk next to the street, unless they are on a dark street with alleyways where a stranger may be lurking. In that case, the man walks on the side next to the entrance to the alleyways.

Long ago, before paved roads, people rode in wagons and horse-drawn carriages along dirt streets that were often wet and muddy, so the gentleman walked next to the street to protect the lady's long, flowing skirts and petticoats from muddy splashes.

Suggestion: Next time you're out walking together, practice this rule. Also, discuss the reasoning behind the rule of the man walking next to the street. Knowing the reason helps us remember the rule.

The age of chivalry is never past, so long as there is a wrong left unredressed on earth.
Charles Kingsley

Upstairs, Downstairs

A gentleman should precede a lady or an elderly person going down stairs. When going up stairs, the gentleman follows. The reason for this rule is safety. The lady may be wearing high heels and might trip going up the stairs, thus the gentleman behind can catch her. The same is true coming down. He should be in front to catch her or an elderly person if they start to fall.

Suggestion: If you have stairs in your house, practice this rule and talk about the reasons for the gentleman's proper place in the climb and descent. If you do not have stairs, perhaps you can practice at church, work, or school.

✦ ✦ ✦ ✦ ✦ ✦ ✦

Manners maketh the man.
William of Wykeham

The Go-Around

It is impolite to walk between two people who are talking face to face or to walk in front of someone speaking to a group. This creates an unwanted distraction and portrays a sense of self-importance. This same rule applies at the grocery store, for example, not stepping between a person and the store shelves unless the other person waves you through. Still, be sure to say "excuse me."

Suggestion: Talk about how you may have felt when someone interrupted your conversation with a friend by walking between the two of you. Someone has said it feels like being knocked off the sidewalk. Maybe your family members have other appropriate descriptions.

Turn not your back to others, especially in speaking; jog not the table or desk on which another reads or writes.
George Washington

Getting It Together

It is polite to move over to let others sit together, if they wish. If you are seated in the middle of a row of empty chairs, for example, and a number of people who are obviously arriving as a group come in, it is best for you to move to the end of the row of chairs so they can stay together.

Suggestion: Talk about being aware of your surroundings and how you can anticipate the needs of others by thinking more of others than yourself. What other settings or situations do these rules of politeness apply to?

A person's pride will humble him,
but a humble spirit will gain honor.
Proverbs 29:23

Part 10
Notes and Letters

Silent gratitude isn't much use to anyone.
G. B. Stern

A Handwritten Letter

With all the electronic ways to communicate, we sometimes forget what a treasure a handwritten note can be. Personal correspondence such as thank-you notes are more important than many people realize. Children as young as three years old should know how to create a thank-you note.

Suggestion: Talk about the different reasons for writing a personal note, such as thank-you notes, sympathy notes, and invitations. You may bring out some of your keepsake notes for show and tell.

The apostle Paul had a handicap; some think it was his eyesight. This may be why he dictated his letters. Yet when he could, he laboriously wrote some of his own postscripts. In Galatians 6:11, he said, "Look at what large letters I have written to you in my own handwriting."

Thank You Notes

All thank-you notes have the following elements: The writer greets the giver—"Dear Evelyn,"—thanks the giver, names the gift, says something nice about it, puts the date in the bottom left corner or the upper right corner, closes the note with "sincerely," "love," or something similar, and signs it with both first and last names, unless the recipient is a close relative. (Make sure the recipient doesn't have to guess who sent it.)

Suggestion: Practice writing a thank-you note. The gift may be as simple as a favor or helping someone do something. Very young children can scribble or draw a picture of the gift, using crayons or markers, and then "sign" or make their mark.

The president of the United States cannot personally accept a gift worth more than $100.00.

Write Now

Personal notes should be written as quickly as possible after the event. Givers should receive a thank-you note within days after the gift is received—two weeks at the most. (One exception would be notes that are written after a very large wedding reception or other celebration. These should be written within one month of the event.) Actually, though, it's never too late to write a thank-you note!

Suggestion: Choose a place where the proper tools such as nice paper, envelopes, pens, pencils, crayons, markers, and stamps are kept. It can be a desk, a tabletop, a drawer, or lap board. Older family members can help the younger ones in writing their notes. Stickers, stencils, and such may make writing notes more fun for them.

*When you give from the heart,
no one has to leave empty-handed.*
Anonymous

Across the Miles

Notes and cards should be written personally because they become handwritten hugs, making the receiver feel loved and special.

Suggestion: See how many specific occasions you can name for writing a note to someone, such as thank-you notes for a birthday, Christmas, or a "just because" gift. There are get-well notes, "bread and butter" notes after an overnight visit, friendship cards, and responses to invitations. What about a note following a special trip or outing? Or a note to a Sunday school teacher or church leader for being a thoughtful, caring friend?

What a wonderful thing is the mail,
capable of conveying across continents
a warm human hand-clasp.

Anonymous

Postal Codes

For social notes, there are some guidelines for buying the correct paper, cards, and envelopes. Each note and card should have its own matching envelope. The envelopes and their notes when folded should be approximately three and a half inches by five inches or a little larger, never smaller. The post office will not accept smaller ones.

Suggestion: Go to a stationery store (or a discount store) and purchase nice notepaper, fold-over notes, and/or blank cards, pencils, pens, markers, and stamps. Include a family address book while you're at it, if you don't already have a good one.

Monograms were created for stationery hundreds of years ago for illiterate members of royalty. King Charlemagne (742-771) was one of the first. He was unable to write his name, so he drew his monogram instead.

A Kindness Received

When a family member is sick and receives gifts, cards, and food, the ailing one should write notes of appreciation as soon as he or she is feeling better. If the illness is prolonged, however, or the person is incapacitated, another family member may write the notes. (Notes should be written even after the giver says, "You don't have to write me a thank-you note.")

Suggestion: Always keep a master list. List the gift and the giver immediately upon arrival, such as "Mrs. Anthony: the chicken soup; Mr. Anders, the novel." It is good if only one or two people in the family are responsible for the list and the notes.

*The deepest need in human nature
is to be appreciated.*
William James

Have a Nice Stay?

A bread and butter note should be written after an overnight visit. If friends exchange sleepovers often, the note is not obligatory, but it is still a nice gesture and it is proper. When you spend at least one night, the note to write is called a "bread and butter" note because meals, lodging, and time were shared.

Suggestion: Practice writing such a letter by addressing the note to the lady of the house (the hostess). Express thanks and say something especially nice about the visit, such as a special meal or a specific activity. You can mention the name of the man of the house in the body of the note.

The Egyptians developed a paper-like substance called "papyrus" 4,000 years ago, made from a reed that grows along the banks of the Nile.

Pushing the Envelope

Every envelope must be properly addressed. In the top left corner, write your own street address on one line with the city, state, and zip code on the second line. Near the center of the envelope, write the full name of the recipient on the first line, the street address on the second line, and the city, state, and zip code on the third line.

At one time, it was proper to indent each line of the recipient's address, but technology has changed that rule because it is difficult for the post office equipment to scan uneven lines.

Suggestion: Write a letter as a family to someone today. Make sure to include and double-check all the elements of proper address. Be sure to remember a stamp.

It's the little things we do or say that make or break the beauty of the average passing day.

Anonymous

True Colors

For serious writing, only black or blue ink on white, off white, or gray paper is appropriate. For casual correspondence, the color of the paper along with stickers, drawings, and such may be the writer's choice, whatever feels most fun to you.

Suggestion: Let each family member write a note, choosing the ink and paper suitable for the occasion. A good sentiment for a condolence is the following: "I am so sorry for your loss, I'm praying for you. (Do not say, "Call me if I can help." Say something like: "May I go to the store for you or pick up the dry cleaning or make some calls for you?")

Never write a letter while you are angry.
Chinese proverb

Be Nice

It is proper to write only positive, complimentary, pleasing words in a note or letter. Part of the reason for this is pure politeness, but also—correspondence can be kept, reread, pasted in a scrapbook, and treasured in many other ways. You never know who may read your note now or years later.

Suggestion: Let each family member write a note for another family member to examine for nice and pleasing words. Only gentle criticism or suggestions are welcomed.

♦ ♦ ♦ ♦ ♦ ♦

The letter we all love to receive is one that carries so much of the writer's personality that she (or he) seems to be sitting beside us, looking at us directly and talking just as she (or he) really would.

Emily Post

Mr. and Mrs. Right

On envelopes, use the proper title (such as Mr. or Mrs.) before the recipient's name, and a title (such as M.D.) after the recipient's name with no title before the name: John Smith, M.D. Do not put two names and titles on one line unless you're writing a married couple.

Suggestion: Talk about the different titles you might use to write people you know, and practice writing them on some inexpensive envelopes. Use Mr., Mrs., Ms., Miss, and Dr. as the most common titles used. If you are writing a medical doctor, write Dr. Sam Bowers or Sam Bowers, M.D. Never use two titles for one person's name. Dr. Sam Bowers, M.D. is incorrect. The abbreviations for junior (Jr.) or senior (Sr.), however, are not considered separate titles. Two married individuals require two titles, such as Dr. and Mrs. Joel Sampson.

More than kisses, letters mingle souls.
John Donne

One and Done

It is proper to put two names in one address line only when the two are married. When people are not married but are living at the same address, their names are listed on two consecutive lines. A married couple's names are connected with "and."

Suggestion: Practice addressing something to a married couple, connecting their names with "and." Then address another envelope to two or more unmarried people living at the same address, with one name and title on the first line and the other name and title listed on the second line. For instance, for two sisters living at the same address: Miss (or Ms.) Joan Adams on one line and Miss (or Ms.) Anne Adams on another line.

*A man will leave his father and
mother and be joined to his wife,
and the two will become one flesh.*
Ephesians 5:31

Full Names Only

On any correspondence, spell names out correctly without abbreviating or using initials, except for junior (or senior), which can be written Jr. and Sr. A person's name is his or her identity and distinguishes one individual from another, even within families.

Suggestion: Talk about the juniors and seniors in your family. Practice writing names correctly using these designations. For instance, if you are a junior, the second, or the third, sign your name this way: Thomas Allen Bowers Jr.

Nephews are named the second (II), while a son is named Junior. Therefore, Thomas Allen Bowers II is named for an uncle. The comma normally used before "Jr." and "Sr." has been dropped in this modern age of computers.

Mastering Manners

A young man is addressed as "Master" until he is in junior high school. After that, he is addressed as "Mr."—or without a title until he is eighteen, the age which designated adulthood in olden times.

Suggestion: Practice writing titles for young boys you know who are younger than junior high age. For instance, you will write Master Joey Wilson. You will write Mr. (abbreviation for Mister) Joe Wilson for Joey's dad.

♦ ♦ ♦ ♦ ♦ ♦ ♦

In an age like ours, which is not given to letter-writing, we forget what an important part it is in people's lives.
Anatole Broyard

Ms. and Mrs.

Address a young lady as Miss until marriage when she becomes known as Mrs. before her husband's name (Mrs. Harry Gibbs). If she does not marry, she usually adopts the title Ms. after age twenty-five, unless she prefers to retain Miss.

Miss is short for *mademoiselle*, French for "young lady." Mrs. is the abbreviation of mistress. Ms. does not reveal the woman's marital status.

Suggestion: Both Mrs. and Ms. are pronounced "miz." (though Mrs. may be pronounced "mis'iz.") Use Ms. any time you use a woman's first name (Ms. Joan Smythe) and any time you do not know the marital status of a woman.

In the 1970s, Ms. was coined for divorced women; therefore, married women preferred Mrs. Today, Ms. is especially useful in business, whether the businesswoman is married or not.

Proper Titles

A divorced woman's title should be Ms. before her first name, followed by her last name—Ms. Alice Winthrop. As a divorcee, she no longer uses her former husband's name. A widow, however, retains her husband's first name for life. She continues to be Mrs. Orman Irving even after her husband dies. As mentioned earlier, a single lady become Ms. at about age 25, unless she prefers to remain a Miss.

Suggestion: Name women you know with each title—Mrs., Ms., and Miss. When writing a divorced woman's name, write Ms. Jane Abbott. Name a widowed lady who retains Mrs. with her husband's full name.

♦ ♦ ♦ ♦ ♦ ♦

A recent U.S. Postal Service study found that personal mail has dropped off by a third, due to "the continuing shift in household preference toward e-mail."

To Type or Not to Type

Only business correspondence should be typed or computer generated. All other forms of communication are better expressed in your own writing, which more clearly demonstrates warmth, charm, and friendliness. A handwritten note or letter has a personal touch that no technology can duplicate.

Suggestion: Discuss handwriting—both your own and that of other family members. But be gentle! If someone's handwriting is barely legible, you may suggest that they print instead and use lots of space for easier reading. Crowded script is a chore to read.

Letters are among the most significant memorial a person can leave behind them.
Johann Wolfgang von Goethe

Down in Front

Did you know there's a proper way to insert your letter into an envelope? Place the open edges of folded stationery in the envelope first, facing down, because doing so makes it easier to read when the paper is lifted from it.

Suggestion: Practice stuffing an envelope properly. Hold the envelope with the open, sticky-side flap facing you. Put the open edges of the folded paper in first so that when the paper is removed and opened, the reader unfolds the paper and easily reads your greeting. Notice how it leads them to see the start of your letter first. Try it the incorrect way, too, and see the difference it makes when you remove it from the envelope.

* , ♦ , ♦ ♦ ♦ , ♦ , ♦

Politeness is to human nature what warmth is to wax.
Arthur Schopenhauer

Monograms

The man's initials on monogrammed stationery are placed straight across. A married woman's stationery lists her given name for the first letter, with the second letter for her married name (in larger script), and then the last letter for her maiden name.

Suggestion: Practice writing monograms for yourself and other family members. Here are some examples: J M H, meaning the lady's married name begins with "M." (The M would be larger than the other initials.) Her husband's monogram is H L M, showing that his last name begins with "M." For men, all the letters are the same size. For children and unmarried ladies, the first, middle, and last name initials should read straight across.

Outcomes rarely turn on grand gestures or the art of the deal, but on whether you've sent a thank-you note.
Bernie Brillstein

Nice to Hear from You

Never begin a note or a letter with an apology because it sets a negative tone for the entire piece of correspondence, no matter what you may say later. Even if you're quite delayed in writing, even if you're genuinely sorry for not having written sooner, even if you're writing to share unpleasant news, remember that a note is always welcome. Start on the bright side.

Suggestion: Practice writing notes with positive, beginning words, such as "It was so nice to see you last week. I hope we can talk again soon; however, I regret that I cannot come to your party next week. It sounds like a lot of fun." Using this as a model, make up your own wording.

Gratitude is the memory of the heart.
Jean Baptiste Massieu

Sympathy Notes

Handwritten letters of condolence or sympathy should be written on plain white or gray paper to show respect to the recipient, not on bright, heavily decorated stationery.

Suggestion: When writing a sympathy note, simply express how sorry you are about the loss of the loved one (or pet, or loss of anything). If it is a loved one, say some good things you remember about the person. Finally, give a specific offer of help, if possible, rather than "Let me know if I can do anything." No need to say a lot. Your gesture will mean more than you know. Perhaps there's one you can write together right now.

All of you should be like-minded and sympathetic, should love believers, and be compassionate and humble.

1 Peter 3:8

Sad to Say

With sympathy or condolence messages, do not use expressions such as "Time heals all wounds," or "He's so much better off." It's almost never appropriate to say, "I know just how you feel." Better not to be overly philosophical at times like these, just compassionate and supportive, letting the person know of your love and concern.

Suggestion: Discuss phrases that might be comforting to a grieving person, such as "I am so sorry for your loss." Perhaps you can recall comforting words you have received when you were sad or in need.

*The very perfection of manners
is not to think about yourself.*
Richard Whately

You're Invited

No matter how informal, an invitation should be acknowledged within one week (or sooner) because the inviter must carry out many plans. We should never want to complicate her schedule by leaving her uncertain of our attendance.

Suggestion: Discuss the reasons why we should answer invitations quickly and the importance of keeping our commitments unless there is an unavoidable reason, such as a death in the family or if we become ill. Be sure your family has a clear understanding of what promises mean in your dealings with others.

Wedding invitations were once engraved with oil-based inks, which dried very slowly. Tissue was inserted between the invitations to prevent smudging. Tissuing is not necessary anymore, but it has become acceptable over time.

R.S.V.P.

When an invitation contains the letters R.S.V.P., we must answer the sender with yes or no, to let them know of our intentions to come or not. These letters are French for *Répondez, s'il vous plaît*, which means "Answer, please" in English.

Suggestion: If a telephone number is listed, you may call with your answer. If the invitation says "Regrets Only," you must reply only if you cannot attend. If the invitation simply has R.S.V.P., you must write your answer, either on your own stationery or on the enclosed response card.

In New Testament times, invitations were issued in two stages: a first, formal request was always refused with thanks. A second with personal badgering was finally accepted.

Margaret Visser

One for All

There is a long-disputed rule on whose name should appear first on a greeting card—the husband or the wife—when one is signing for both. Some say the signer's name should come first. Others say the signer's name should come last. Today, you may sign a card either way: Mary and Bill Alders or Bill and Mary Alders. Both are acceptable.

Suggestion: Discuss your preferences with the customary "signer" for the family, making a decision about whose name should be written first on a birthday card or other family greeting card. One nice solution is to have individual family members sign their own names.

We look for the designer's name on the dress, the writer's name on the book, and our own names on anything in print—as long as it's not a speeding ticket, or on a "Wanted" poster!
Peggie Bohanon

First and Last

Always sign your first and last name on any correspondence unless you're writing a family member or close relative. You may feel the recipient should know who you are by your first name only, but you do not want the intended recipient to wonder which Alissa or which Reed you are.

Suggestion: Talk about the courtesy of writing both first and last names. Practice signing your first and last name. Out of courtesy and to make sure the recipient knows who you are, sign Alissa Haggerty or Reed Alverson.

A good name is to be chosen over great wealth;
favor is better than silver and gold.
Proverbs 22:1

Part 11
Fine Dining

Manners are a sensitive awareness of the feelings of others. If you have that awareness, you have good manners, no matter which fork you use.

Emily Post

Learned Behavior

Because no one is born with good manners, we all must learn how to eat properly to avoid embarrassing others and ourselves. Good table manners build our self-confidence.

Praise good efforts, no matter how small. Mealtime should be pleasant to promote good digestion, good health, and good harmony. Never embarrass other family members by scolding them about their eating habits in public.

Suggestion: Try to have a family meal once a day or once a week, if possible. Choose one or two rules of good manners to practice each day or each week. Rewards are nice.

You may have been born a princess,
but you have to learn to be a lady.
Queen of England (to one of her granddaughters)

Wait a Minute

At a banquet or a large dinner where the tables are end to end, you should wait only for the four or five people around you to be served before you begin eating. At a round table of six, eight, or even ten, it is proper to wait until all those seated have been served their food.

Suggestion: Talk about the reasons for the rule about mass seating and round table seating. For instance, if you wait for long tables of people to be served, your food may get stone cold; whereas, with a round table, you are face to face in an intimate situation. It would make you look ravenous to begin eating too quickly.

The word "banquet," originally meant a very small meal. The word has evolved into today's meaning of an elaborate feast.

Margaret Visser

Stand and Deliver

At meals, everyone should stand behind his or her chair until the whole group is ready to pull out their chairs and sit (unless the hostess tells you to sit before she arrives at the table.) By waiting, you show respect for the hostess and others, as well as showing self-control in restraining your appetite.

Suggestion: At your next mealtime, let each family member stand behind his or her chair until everyone is ready to be seated, allowing the feminine members to sit first. Talk about the importance of this—and why it's often not followed in many settings today as it should be.

Make no show of taking great delight in your victuals. Feed not with greediness.
George Washington

Sitting Pretty

At the table, a gentleman pulls out the chair for the lady on his right, who slides in from the right side of her chair. The men do not sit down until the hostess is seated. If there is no gentleman to seat the lady on a gentleman's left, he should seat her also.

Suggestion: Let the gentlemen in the family practice pulling out the chairs for the ladies at the table. The ladies will slide in from the right side of the chair, then grip the sides of the chair to help the gentleman move the chair forward.

He himself will seat them, put on an apron,
and serve them as they sit and eat.
Luke 12:37 (NLT)

Seated with Style

There is a proper way for a lady to sit. She steps to the front of the chair with the back of her knees touching the front edge of the chair. Then she lowers herself into the chair (without projecting her derriere). If on a stage or platform, she sits on the front of the chair without leaning back. She does not cross her legs, but may cross her ankles.

Suggestion: Have the ladies practice standing in front of a chair, lowering themselves to the chair cushion and crossing their ankles.

It's nice to be important,
but it's more important to be nice.
John Cassis

Three Meals

There are three styles of dining: informal (or family dining), buffet, and formal, which you experience in an elegant restaurant, at a banquet, or in someone's home. At informal, family-style meals, diners pass bowls of food around. At buffets, food is presented on a serving table where guests fill their plates and often eat standing up. At formal meals, the hostess or servers bring the food and beverage in from the kitchen on individual plates, serving each diner individually from the left.

Suggestion: Let each family member describe each of the three styles of dining.

* * * * * * *

The nineteenth-century term "buffet meal" meant that a meal was laid out on the sideboard. Diners helped themselves, carrying their food to the table. Today, the "buffet" usually holds the family china.

Margaret Visser

Place Settings

A place setting, also called a "cover," is the arrangement of plates, forks, knives, glasses, and spoons on the table for each diner. The placements are based on when and how each piece will be used. To begin dining, always start from the outside and move inward, choosing the proper fork, glass, or spoon in the order in which the food is eaten. If salad is the first dish served, there will be a salad fork to the far left of the place setting.

Suggestion: Examine and talk about place settings you see in magazines or on television. They will not always be correct. Practice setting your own table.

The origin of the term "covers" for place settings is from the wrappings or napkin that went around the king's spoon and knife, placed there to protect him from poison.

Place Setting with Salad

Formal Place Setting

Eating at Home

The informal (or family) place setting should have a dinner plate in the center with a knife and a spoon on the right of the plate and a fork on the left of the plate (all with the points of the handles about ½ to 1 inch from the edge of the table). A glass goes above the plate near the tip of the knife blade. The napkin goes on the left of the fork (or forks). The placement order is based on the order of the meal—which utensil will be needed first. (Remember, start with an outside utensil.)

Suggestion: Let each family member take turns setting the table properly.

A man finds out what is meant by "a spitting image" when he tries to feed cereal to his infant.

Anonymous

Left-Handed Forks?

Families should not reverse the place setting for a left-handed eater because, unfortunately, we live in a right-handed world. Reversing the silverware at home to try accommodating a left-handed eater will make life more difficult for these children once they are older and eating away from family.

Suggestion: Guide your left-handed children in learning to maneuver a place setting arranged for right-handed people, but never discourage them from using their dominant hand. Talk about ways in which we must all adapt in one way or another to various situations in life. Discuss some examples from your own life where you had to adjust to your surroundings in a public setting.

Bumper sticker: Lefties have rights, too.

Extra Dental Work

If you wear a dental appliance, remove it privately before you get to the table. Removing your appliance may be a normal part of your day, but others do not want to see you do it. When away from home, put the appliance in a pocket or a purse. (Wrapping it in tissue paper or a napkin invites the disaster of losing it or having it thrown away with the trash.)

Suggestion: Practice removing any appliance before coming to the table. Secure it in its proper place—perhaps in a container in the bathroom.

Reports continue to come in about a parent and student digging through the school cafeteria garbage trying to find a lost $300 retainer.

Too Much? Too Little?

If you are the guest of someone in a restaurant, ask your host to please suggest something from the menu or tell you what he or she plans to order. That way, you will know your host's price range.

If the host will not suggest something or tell you what he or she is having, simply order something in the mid-price range of the menu.

Suggestion: Talk about the reason for not ordering the cheapest thing or the most extravagant thing on the menu. (The first option makes the host look cheap, and the second option may be more than the host can afford).

The pleasure of eating something because it is expensive has absolutely nothing to do with the taste of good cuisine.

X. Marcel Boulestin

I'd Recommend

When you are treating someone to lunch or dinner at a restaurant, you should suggest an item from the menu, which then gives your guest (or guests) an idea of what you are expecting to pay. If your budget is indeed limited, mention your selection, such as chicken or hamburger (over the sirloin), but if you have an unlimited budget, simply tell them to order whatever they like.

Suggestion: Talk about experiences you have had as a guest when you didn't know what to order because someone else was paying. What did your host do (or not do) to try putting you at ease in a situation like that?

They take great pride in making their dinner cost much; I take my pride in making my dinner cost so little.
Henry David Thoreau

Seating Order

When your family goes to a restaurant where a hostess seats you, Mom follows the hostess with the children following her, and Dad trails along as the last one in the lineup. If there is no one to seat the family, Dad goes first with the children behind him, and Mom follows them to the table. The ladies, of course, are seated first in both incidences.

Another rule says that the gentleman should lead the way whenever there is danger or the unknown. In the case of being seated for a meal, the "unknown" may warrant the father to go first.

Suggestion: Plan an outing to a nice restaurant for the family to practice being seated in the proper order.

The state of Connecticut has a law requiring restaurant owners to offer nose-blowing sections to their patrons.

Purse Positions

Do not place purses, briefcases, or hats on a tabletop—nothing but food, drink, and eating utensils. The best place to put your purse is in your lap (In fact, ladies should carry a small one when eating out, if possible). Place briefcases or a large purse between your feet.

Suggestion: Talk about where you can put personal items when eating out, such as on a vacant chair or in your lap, if possible. Talk about why putting things on the floor is not a good idea unless there is no other place. Putting purses and briefcases on the floor can cause someone to trip over them.

Now, Grandma, we say the blessing.
We chew with our mouth closed. We use our
fork—and we don't put our foot on the table.
A precocious four-year-old

Saying Grace

At each meal, the host or hostess should say the blessing (grace) or ask an appointed person to say the prayer. Some families take turns. In other families, the father or head of the house always does the honors.

Suggestion: Before anyone touches anything on the table, let everyone bow their head for prayer after the hostess is seated. Unless the head of the family always says the prayer, let family members take turns at alternate meals saying the blessing.

* ✦ * ✦ * ✦ * ✦ * ✦

We Christians call it "saying the blessing" or "saying grace" before our meals. Strictly speaking, a benediction ("blessing") is said at the beginning, and "grace" is a thanking, at the end of the meal.

Napkin Placement

Immediately after the meal has been blessed, the hostess should lead the other diners in placing their large, cloth dinner napkins in their laps, opening the napkins halfway before placing them in their laps with the fold pointing toward her knees. Men place a napkin across one leg.

Suggestion: During family meals, practice placing the napkin properly in the lap. Practice lifting the napkin at the folded edge, dabbing the corners of the mouth, not swiping side to side. When the napkin is replaced in the lap with the fold toward the knees, any smudges will be on the top side of the napkin and not on your clothes.

Keep your fingers clean and, when foul, wipe them on a corner of your table napkin.
George Washington

Napkin Rings

When you sit down to a meal and see a napkin ring, slip the napkin out and lay the ring down on the table to your left.

Suggestion: Napkin rings are mostly decorative today, but they have a very interesting origin you can talk about. Long ago, each family member had his or her own distinctive napkin ring. Since napkins were used at more than one meal, diners wanted to make sure they had their own previously-used napkin and not someone else's, hence the need for a napkin ring.

*Too many people just eat to consume calories.
Try dining for a change.*
John Walters

Little Napkins

Paper napkins and small luncheon napkins should be fully opened before being placed in the lap, simply because they are so small even when opened completely. With disposable napkins like these, it is still proper to place them in your lap while eating, not on the table or beside your plate.

Never put a used napkin in your plate. Always place it to your left on the table any time you leave.

Suggestion: Practice opening a small paper napkin completely and placing it in your lap. (Remember, gentlemen place the napkin across one leg.) Help those who may be having trouble keeping the napkin in place.

In an Asian restaurant, use the hot towel offered. Return it to the tray it came on or place it on the table beside your plate.

Watch the Hostess

At an informal meal, after the hostess has placed the napkin properly in her lap, she should pick up the proper fork or spoon to begin eating the meal. The first utensil used at informal meals is usually the salad fork, the dinner fork, or the dinner knife and fork, depending on what she plans to eat first: salad, vegetables, or meat.

Suggestion: Practice watching the hostess and picking up the first fork or spoon you use, holding it like a pencil.

The world was my oyster,
but I used the wrong fork.
Oscar Wilde

Missing Silverware

If you discover you are missing a piece of silverware, simply say, "I seem to be missing my steak knife." You can make this request without being rude or drawing unnecessary attention to the mistake. At home, you should briefly excuse yourself and get one for yourself from the utensil drawer, without making negative comments.

Suggestion: Talk about why you should get a missing piece of silverware for yourself at home. Discuss what you would do if a guest drops his knife, fork, or spoon. (Get him another one.)

*During the nineteenth century, the knife was
downplayed, used as little as possible,
and put aside when it was not in use.*
Margaret Visser

Soup Spoons

Creamy or thin soup is eaten the same way whether it is the main dish or simply the first course. The proper method is this: Hold the soup spoon in a horizontally level position, skimming the top of the soup while scooping it away from yourself. Take the soup spoon across the back rim of the bowl to catch any drips before taking the spoon to your mouth, still holding it in a horizontally level position and sipping (not slurping) from the side of the spoon.

Suggestion: Serve soup at your next meal so you can practice. The proper method of eating soup prevents spills and drips, especially because soup spoons are usually large and round, making them difficult to put into your mouth.

An easy rhyme to help remember how to eat soup: As the ship goes out to sea, I scoop my soup away from me.

Thick Soup

Chunky soups are eaten by taking the spoonful across the back rim of the bowl to catch drips—just as you do with thin or creamy soups—but you do not sip from the side of the spoon. Place the bowl of the spoon into your mouth just far enough to take the veggies or other ingredients off with your lips, without opening your mouth any wider than necessary.

Suggestion: Prepare your favorite stew or chunky soup and practice taking the spoon across the back rim of the bowl, pointing it to the lips, then taking the chunky pieces off the spoon without opening your mouth widely.

Manners are noises you don't make when eating soup.
Anonymous

Dribs and Drabs

Dab your mouth with your napkin before and after you drink from a glass or cup to prevent getting a smudge on the rim of the glass, while at the same time removing water, milk, tea, or whatever beverage you're having from your upper lip.

Suggestion: Practice using the napkin before and after taking a drink. Remember, dabbing doesn't mean rubbing or wiping, just a gentle touching and spotting at the corners of the mouth. Talk about why this is the proper method.

Do not drink more than two or three times during the meal, and wipe your lips with a napkin after each sip.
Desiderius Erasmus

Sweet Tea

At an informal, family meal, any unsweetened tea or other beverage should be sweetened after the blessing is invoked and the napkin placed.

Suggestion: Let someone closest to the sugar bowl pick it up. It should have its own serving spoon. Scoop some sugar or take a packet of artificial sweetener. Sprinkle the sugar or packet contents into the glass and stir the beverage as noiselessly as possible. Place the empty paper on the little dish under the glass or on the bread and butter plate. If there is no other place for the sweetener packet, tuck the torn-off part of the envelope into the open end and lay the envelope neatly on the table.

There is a difference between dining and eating.
Dining is an art.
Yuan Mei

Tea Spoon

After preparing and stirring a beverage, never lay the spoon on the table nor leave it protruding upward in the glass. The iced tea spoon is the only eating utensil you can prop. All other implements are placed securely on a plate at any time they are not in the diner's hand, because used silverware should never be put back on the table or tablecloth.

Suggestion: Practice inverting the iced tea spoon with the bowl turned downward. Place the tip of the bowl of the spoon on the rim of a plate, with the long handle pointing to the right. You may also place a used iced tea spoon on an empty packet of sweetener. (A coffee spoon should be placed on the saucer beneath the cup.)

Until as recently as 1855, diners did not have individual glasses; often drink was imbibed from a single cup, passed around.

Margaret Visser

Juicy Propositions

A slice of lemon or lime on the rim of a glass should be squeezed or simply removed from the glass. Never leave anything on the rim of a glass. To squeeze a slice of lemon or lime, take it with one hand to squeeze, while covering it with the other hand to prevent squirting juice in someone's eye.

Suggestion: Talk about times you may have been squirted with lemon juice or have perhaps squirted juice on someone else—accidentally, of course. Then practice following the above directions about squeezing a lemon slice.

The pleasant hours of our life are all connected by a more or less tangible link, with some memory of the table.
Charles Pierre Monselet

Drinking Glasses

The glasses and cups are always on your right; therefore, it is most practical and safe to fill them from the right. The hostess or server who fills the beverage pieces does so without lifting them from the table. For cleanliness sake, no one's hands should ever touch the rim of a glass or cup.

The glasses are placed on the tabletop in descending order. In other words, the first glass on your right should be the beverage you drink first. (Cups and saucers are usually brought with the dessert.)

Suggestion: Practice serving beverages properly by leaving the glass or cup on the table and pouring from the pitcher directly into the beverage holder.

Drink not nor talk with your mouth full;
neither gaze about you while you are drinking.
George Washington

Spill Proofing

To pick up and drink from a stemmed glass, place your thumb on the stem while supporting the lower portion of the bowl of the glass with some of your other fingers. It is not proper to hold a stemmed glass as you would a tumbler. Before picking up your glass, wipe your mouth so you don't leave a smear on the glass. Do not swizzle your beverage.

Suggestion: Select all the different types of glasses in your cabinet and let each family member practice holding them properly. Demonstrate what can happen (without actually breaking anything!) by holding glasses in not-so-secure ways.

Drink not too leisurely nor yet too hastily.
George Washington

Curled Pinkies

Here's the mystery of the raised, crooked pinkie: A tea cup handle is held with the index finger through the handle, with the thumb above the handle and the third finger under the handle. The thumb and the third finger are both used for support. The remaining two fingers simply curl naturally.

The raised pinkie myth does not denote social sophistication but is merely a proper way of holding a teacup, as long as it's not done too pretentiously.

Suggestion: Practice holding a teacup in the correct manner, as described above.

By the age of ten, children should be reasonably well-socialized human beings, aware of almost all of the important tenets of good manners, lacking only the adult polish.
Letitia Baldridge

Drink Requests

While it is rude to refuse any food that someone sets in front of you, you may politely refuse beverages, especially alcoholic beverages. Drinking is a personal issue. It is not polite, however, to make disparaging remarks about the beverage or to condemn those who are drinking. Simply say, "No, thank you." If the beverage is already on the table, simply ignore it and drink water.

Suggestion: Talk about the reasons certain individuals might have for not drinking a beverage, such as allergic reactions, faith-based reasons, or health issues. For instance, diabetics must refrain from too much sweet drink, wine, and such.

We are fighting Germany, Austria, and drink, and as far as I can see, the greatest of these three deadly foes is drink.
David Lloyd George

Salad Days

It is proper these days to cut a salad with a knife and fork because we use stainless steel; therefore, the vinegar will not tarnish the metal, as it did in the past when utensils were more commonly made of inferior metals. Also, restaurants often serve such huge wedges of lettuce that a salad would be inedible if diners could not cut it up.

Suggestion: Practice cutting a salad by holding the knife and fork in the same way as you would when cutting any other food (see #291).

It takes four men to dress a salad: a wise man for the salt, a madman for the pepper, a miser for the vinegar, and a spendthrift for the oil.

Anonymous

Case of the Missing Salad

If you go to a banquet or large dinner where the salad is already on the table, and someone mistakenly gets your salad (which should be to the left of your forks), there is a way to politely get one for yourself. Looking around, you should be able to spot an extra salad, uneaten. Simply say, "I seem to be missing a salad. May I have that one?"

Suggestion: Practicing this rule at home should be easy. Just let one family member reach for the wrong salad (or anything else, like your roll plate or your dessert) and let the one without ask the question above.

To remember a successful salad is generally to remember a successful dinner.
George Ellwanger

Chip and Dip

If chips and dip are served, never "double dip." That is, never dip a chip in the bowl, eat from it, and then dip the half-eaten chip in the bowl again. The reason for this rule is obvious—germs.

Suggestion: Practice breaking a large chip in two pieces or choosing a chip small enough to dip and put into your mouth all at one time (without stuffing, of course). Finish the dipped chip you're eating before reaching for another one.

Potato chips were invented in 1853 by a New York chef trying to rile his dinner guest, who had complained that the french fries were too thick.

Cleansing Your Palate

Your palate is the roof of your mouth, where you discern your sense of taste. To cleanse the palate before the main course, sorbet may be served. It comes in a small compote on a small plate with a very small spoon. Made of frozen fruit juice, sorbet is served (not ordered) just before the main course, never at any other time, and usually only at very expensive dinners. Sorbet never contains milk, which coats the palate.

Suggestion: Try making up some sorbet or purchasing it (not sherbet) and serving it with dinner.

In 1989, the Japanese emperor announced that for the first time in history, there would be no required food-tasting before every royal meal.

Margaret Visser

Sorbet the Right Way

Sorbet is eaten the same way as creamy soup. Use the little spoon that comes with the sorbet to scoop up some of the fruit flavor and take the spoon across the back rim of the compote. Never leave the spoon handle protruding upward from the compote. Place it on the little plate beneath your sorbet any time the spoon is not in your hand. This prevents unwanted, unsightly accidents.

Suggestion: Look online or in a cookbook for a sorbet recipe. Sorbet usually has only two or three ingredients, briefly cooked, then frozen before serving. Involve everyone in choosing the one you'd like to create.

In New Jersey, it is against the law to slurp soup.

Pass to the Right

According to Emily Post, food served family-style is passed around the table to the right (counterclockwise) for efficiency. After diners help themselves to the food on the dish or platter in front of them, they pass that dish to the person sitting on their right.

Suggestion: Prepare your favorite bread or rolls (or use store-bought rolls) for your next meal. Practice passing them to the right all the way around the table. After that, simply pass them in the most convenient direction to reach the diner who requests them next.

Mind your manners so no one will have to mind your bad manners.

Anonymous

Hot Plate

With hot or heavy dishes, the diner serves himself and then sets the platter or bowl on the tabletop (or hot pad) to his right. That way, the next diner to the right can serve himself without holding onto the hot or heavy dish. That diner then sets the food on his right in turn.

Suggestion: Practice passing a bowl or platter to the one seated on your right by picking up the bowl and placing it on the tabletop (or hot pad) so your tablemate can serve himself and pass it along the same way.

Apparently to prevent their use as toothpicks, it became illegal in France in 1669 for cutlers to make pointed dinner knives or for innkeepers to lay them on their tables.

Margaret Visser

Accident Insurance

When served in courses, each dish is served from the left to prevent a collision between the diner reaching for a beverage or a bowl of hot soup. Imagine making the mistake of serving hot soup from the right as a diner reaches for the beverage. That could be a dining disaster!

Suggestion: Take turns serving the family, one course at a time. For instance, serve a salad from the left to each diner at the table. Then remove that plate from the diner's right and serve the main dish from the left.

"Serenely full," the epicure would say,
"Fate cannot harm me, I have dined today."
Sydney Smith

The Salt, Please?

Pass food and condiments to the right only on their first journey around the table. After that, pass them the shortest direction to the diner who requests it. And never gesture with your fork, spoon, or knife, as if talking with them when making your request for a plate or condiment to be passed.

Suggestion: See who can name the most condiments. These include butter, ketchup, salt, pepper, and sugar, among others. Also, practice passing the condiments at every meal. It is your responsibility to pass whatever you find in front of you. Encourage one another to be helpful and gracious in this.

Dining is and always was
a great artistic opportunity.
Frank Lloyd Wright

Salt and Pepper

Always pass salt and pepper shakers together. Think of them as a married pair. When you are finished using them, you should set both of them beside you on the tabletop for the next diner to pick up, use, and pass on.

An interesting story about the salt and pepper involves Mr. J.C. Penney, who founded the chain of department stores bearing his name. He would not hire people who salted or peppered their food before tasting it. He felt such people were impulsive and not good prospective employees.

Suggestion: Practice passing the salt and pepper shakers together, even when someone asks for only one of them.

It is a true saying that a man must eat a peck of salt with his friend before he knows him.

Miguel de Cervantes

Care for Another?

At all informal or family meals, diners should watch their tablemates, anticipating anything they might need to be passed to them. Eating in the company of others should be a pleasure and privilege where we look out for one another's needs.

Suggestion: Talk about the courtesy of asking fellow diners if you may pass something. Practice by placing at least one item in front of each family member so they may pass it to another family member during the meal. It is polite to say something like the following: "Sarah, you seem to have finished your roll. Would you care for another one?" If no one asks, Sarah may simply request one.

Better a dry crust with peace than a house full of feasting with strife.
Proverbs 17:1

Ask and Receive

It is proper to ask for something on the table that is out of your reach, although you should wait if asking for the item or dish interrupts conversation or otherwise distracts. It is very impolite to simply reach across others to retrieve what you need. Besides, you might spill or knock something over.

Suggestion: Practice requesting something to be passed to you, being sure to say "please" and "thank you." The proper way is to say, for instance, "Dad, please pass the salt and pepper."

In dining, as distinguished from mere feeding,
the palate and stomach never ask the hand,
"What are you giving us?"
Ambrose Bierce

One Way or the Other

Both American and Continental styles of eating are correct, but you must choose one style. It is not proper to switch back and forth between the two. Holding your silverware incorrectly draws undue attention and may cause embarrassing mishaps.

The American way shifts the fork after cutting with it (tines downward) from the left hand to the right for carrying food to the mouth with the tines turned upward now. (Tines downward for holding the food to be cut; tines upward for carrying food to your mouth.) The Continental style keeps the knife in the right hand while eating with the fork in the left, tines turned downward, never upward.

Suggestion: Discuss whether you eat American or Continental style.

*On the Continent, people have good food;
in England, people have good table manners.*
George Mikes

The Cutting Edge

To prepare for cutting food with a knife and fork, open your hands, palms up. Place the fork with the tines up in your open left palm. Next, lay the knife across your right palm with the sharp edge facing left. Secure each with a thumb placed over each handle. Grasping the fork and knife, turn your hands over, pressing the left index finger on the back of the fork with tines pointing downward. Point your right index finger on the back of the knife, toward the point. Your thumbs will be on the underside of the fork and knife with a firm, secure grip. Remember to keep your elbows close to your side as you cut.

Suggestion: Practice makes perfect.

After its introduction in the eleventh-century, the fork took eight centuries to become a utensil employed universally in the West.
Margaret Visser

The Proper Way to Hold the Fork and Knife for Cutting

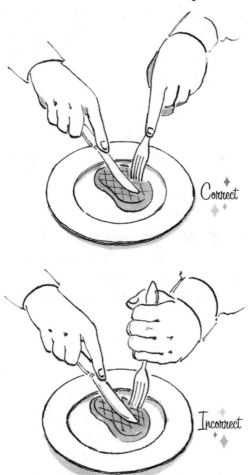

Correct

Incorrect

American Style

For both American and Continental styles, you must always cut your meat by holding your fork with the point of the handle in your palm and the fork tines (prongs) turned downward, securing the piece of food while you cut.

To eat American style, lay the knife down across the upper part of your plate with the cutting edge toward the center of the plate. Switch the fork to your right hand, putting food on your fork (tines upward) into your mouth.

Suggestion: Learn and help other family members hold and eat with their silverware properly, using the American style, being careful not to hold your knife and fork in a fist with the fork hand standing upright.

Neither eat your bread with a knife.
Neither find fault with what you eat.
George Washington

The Fashionable Fork

To hold the fork properly in American style, you must switch your fork to your right (or dominant) hand after cutting the food, holding it like a pencil between your index and middle finger, secured by your thumb. Place the knife across the upper part of the plate with the sharp edge facing you. Eat with the fork tines pointing upward.

Suggestion: Practice holding the fork properly, being careful never to hold it like a shovel. Keep trying until you can do it naturally, without thinking hard.

The Anglo-Saxons used forks as early as the seventh century. Then the religious rulers said they resembled the devil's pitchfork, and they disappeared for several hundred years.

Margaret Visser

Small Bites

It is proper to cut only one or two bites of food at a time because cutting more than this amount makes your plate look messy. Not only that, it causes your food to get cold more quickly.

Suggestion: Practice cutting one or two bites and eating them before cutting any more. With your knife, cut your food in front of the fork. Do not saw back and forth. Gently pull the knife across the meat toward the edge of the table.

To make a mistake is only an error in judgment, but to adhere to it when it is discovered shows infirmity of character.

Dale E. Turner

Blade In

For safety's sake, always lay a table knife down with the cutting edge turned toward the center of the plate. It keeps the blade from being exposed, perhaps grazing someone's hand as they reach for something. When setting the table, the cutting edge is on the right of and in line with the plate.

Suggestion: Practice cutting and laying your knife down properly. Give gentle critiques to family members who forget and turn their knife the wrong way. It may take a while before this becomes a habit.

Practice puts brains in your muscles.
Sam Snead

Left or Right

In both the American and Continental styles of eating, the knife always goes in the dominant hand for cutting. (If you are left handed, for example, put the knife in your left hand and your fork in the right.)

It is gracious, too, when you are with people of other cultures to try learning their way of eating, as with chopsticks.

Suggestion: Make sure each family member is holding his or her utensils properly, being careful not to scrape or make loud noises as they're cutting.

Measurements:
1 smidgen=a teensy bit; 3 teensy bits=1 pinch;
4 pinches=1 little bit; 4 little bits=1 middlin' amount;
3 middlin' amounts=1 right smart;
5 right smarts=1 whole heap.

Continental Style

In Continental style eating, the knife remains in the right hand, and the fork (with tines downward) remains in the left hand throughout the meal. Never lay them down except to take a sip of a beverage or to butter a roll. Some people find it more efficient to eat using the Continental style, keeping the knife in the right hand and eating from the inverted fork in the left with food on the back of the fork.

Suggestion: Let any family member who wants to learn the Continental style spend time practicing it. Offer them patience and only gentle critiques.

The dinner table is the center for the teaching and practicing not just of table manners but of conversation, consideration, tolerance, family feeling, and just about all the other accomplishments of polite society."
Judith Martin (Miss Manners)

Two-Handed Eating

Eating Continental style means you must use your knife to push your peas onto the back of the fork tines for eating, because in the Continental style you cannot shift the fork from your left hand to your right hand.

Suggestion: Try eating Continental style by using your knife to push a morsel on the back of your fork with the tines turned downward. If you have cream potatoes, they can help keep the food on your fork. It takes lots and lots of practice to eat Continental style consistently. Most Americans choose the American way.

I eat my peas with honey—I've done it all my life. It makes the peas taste funny, but it keeps them on my knife.
An old rhyme

Ten to Four

In American style, when you finish a course or the meal, think of your plate as a clock, placing your knife and fork in a ten minutes to four o'clock (3:50) position on the plate with the points toward the ten and the handles toward the four on a clock.

In Continental style, do the same except leave the tines of the fork turned downward. Both knife and fork should be parallel. If food is piled near the top of your plate, move it down with your fork before placing knife and fork so the utensils don't fall off when the hostess or server picks up your plate.

Suggestion: Practice placing your utensils on your plate with the knife slightly above the fork.

Correct Placement of Utensils

Loosen Up

It is very bad manners to hold one's spoon or fork in a fist in the dominant hand, with the palm of the hand covering the top side of the handle. This makes it appear as though you are eating with a shovel, not a dining utensil.

Suggestion: Practice holding every spoon and every fork just as you hold a pencil—delicately, not in bold and abrupt motions that noisily draw attention to yourself.

Early dinner-table forks were generally two-pronged, large, and used mostly to help in cutting and serving, not eating. Our carving forks still keep the size, shape, and original function.

Margaret Visser

Not My Taste

If you cannot eat something, whatever your reason, move the food around a little with your fork or spoon. Do not sit with your arms folded and with a disgusted look on your face. Your fellow diners will feel uncomfortable and wonder why you are not eating.

Suggestion: Talk about why it's not hypocritical to pretend to eat something. (Others at the table may not even realize you are not eating. After all, sharing a meal together is the most important thing, not stuffing yourself as though it were your last meal on earth.)

You are what you eat. For example, if you eat garlic you may be forced to become a hermit.

Anonymous

Mouth Closed

Do not talk with your mouth full of food because it is most unattractive, not to mention unappetizing to others at the table. Chew slowly, chew quietly, and be careful not to attract undue attention to yourself.

Suggestion: Have a contest or play a game in which your family sees who can chew with their mouth closed and not get caught talking with food in their mouth. You might like to place a mirror on the table to show what he or she looks like when breaking the rule of waiting to swallow before talking.

Let your lips be tightly closed while eating.
Ecclesiastes 12:4 (TLB)

Waiting on an Answer

If someone asks you a question while you are chewing, hold up your index finger to indicate that you need a minute to finish swallowing before you answer. This will let the person know that you've heard him and aren't ignoring him, but you want to honor him by not speaking with your mouth full.

Suggestion: Let each family member practice holding up one finger to signal that he or she needs a few moments to finish a bite before commenting or answering the question.

John Doe spends some twenty thousand hours chewing and swallowing food, more than eight hundred days and nights of steady eating. The mere contemplation of this fact is upsetting enough.

M. F. K. Fisher

Eat and Drink

Swallow completely any bite of food in your mouth before drinking from a beverage container so that you will not dribble food or water as you drink nor get unsightly food on the rim of your glass or cup. This also helps to ensure that you won't get choked on any large, unchewed portion.

Suggestion: Practice swallowing your food and dabbing your mouth with your napkin so you won't leave ugly smudges on the glass or cup.

Some of us are gourmets, some gourmands,
and a good many take their images precooked
out of a can and swallow them down whole,
absent-mindedly and with little relish.
W. H. Auden

Sit Up Straight

Correct posture at the dining table is important because a sloppy, leaning, or propping position at the table makes us look lazy. Slouching and slumping also do not lend themselves to good digestion and healthy muscle development. This is not just proper at the dinner table but in any setting.

Suggestion: If you are one who sits improperly at the table, admit that this is an area needing work. Let every family member practice sitting up straight with their feet firmly on the floor and with elbows close to their sides. That way no one will "elbow" the diner next to him.

Lean not on the table. Lay not your arm but only your hand upon the table.
George Washington

Hard Going Down

Your fingers should never go into your mouth except to retrieve a bone, which is a safety rule. If you must remove something from your mouth, you should take it out with the same piece of silverware you used while putting it in. Hide the offending morsel under something on your plate—like the parsley, for instance. Do not place it under your plate because it will only reappear when that plate is removed.

Suggestion: Practice by covering your mouth with your left hand while using your fork in your dominant hand to remove something, such as a piece of tough gristle. When eating stewed fruit, remove a seed or pit with the spoon.

Put not your meat to your mouth with your knife; neither spit forth the stones of any fruit pie upon a dish nor cast anything under the table.
George Washington

All Hands on Deck

Never touch your head or scratch your body at a dining table. Not only is it disgusting, you might contaminate your food. If you have a persistent itch or your hair needs rearranging, excuse yourself to the bathroom and take care of it in private. Remember that you are always making an impression when you are out in public.

Suggestion: Discuss how it feels to see someone scratching his body or combing and moving his hair around while food is on the table. Be sure to watch for this at your family dinner table, and correct it when necessary.

* * *

Whoever one is, and wherever one is,
one is always in the wrong if one is rude.
Maurice Baring

No Need to Reach

Do not reach across the dining table for the condiments, a dish, or a platter. It is rude to reach your arm in front of someone. You might knock something over, spill it, and make a mess. Quietly ask someone to pass you the butter or whatever you need.

Suggestion: Practice asking for something to be passed to you at the dining table. Instruct everyone to resist the temptation to reach for it themselves. Remind them that part of enjoying a meal is found in interacting and serving each other.

The forerunner of the modern placemat was the "doily," named after a seventeenth-century London draper called Mr. D'Oyley.

Margaret Visser

Keep It Clean

Never pick your teeth, use dental floss, or lick your fingers or silverware at the table (or anywhere else in public, for that matter) because this is disgusting. If you have a problem tooth or something stuck in your braces, excuse yourself to the bathroom to take care of the problem.

Suggestion: Discuss the rudeness of seeing someone do any of the above and how meals are meant to be shared in pleasant company encouraging good digestion.

*Hot things, sharp things, sweet things,
cold things—all rot the teeth, and make them
look like old things.*
Benjamin Franklin

Speaking of Manners

Do not wave your fork, knife, spoon, or anything else around in the air as you talk. You could accidentally injure someone, and no one wants to watch your food-laden fork waving around near them. If you must talk with your hands, do so discreetly with empty hands held close to your face.

Suggestion: Discuss how it looks and feels to see someone pointing or waving a utensil around and why this is such bad manners. What could you do to help yourself remember this rule or make it harder to break?

Long ago, men used sticks or sharp knives to spear a chunk of meat. Since the men liked to flail their utensils around as they talked, they established this rule: Keep the sharp edge of the knife turned toward the person using it. Otherwise, they might nick their neighbor in the nose.

Margaret Visser

Dinner Conversation

Among the things you should avoid talking about at the dinner table are your allergies or certain foods you dislike. Visualizing food that someone detests or that causes them to itch or break out in hives can ruin a good appetite.

Suggestion: Consider family members who have a weak stomach. Talk about why you should refrain from talking about personal problems (such as being considerate of others' feelings and sensitivities). Discuss the kind of topics that make for good dinner conversation.

The citrus-flavored soda 7UP was created in 1929. "7" was selected because the original container held seven ounces. "UP" indicated the direction of the bubbles.

Topical Study

When visiting at the dinner table, do not talk about diets, politics, road kill, or any other offensive or argumentative subject. These subjects ruin digestion and run the risk of offending others. Never say "yuck" or make other unpleasant sounds, but attempt to be gracious and cordial.

Suggestion: Talk about the nuances of this rule, such as finding another time and place for a family discussion where opinions differ. While it is all right to mention what political party you support, it is never appropriate to discuss party differences. You may talk about your church, but be careful not to offend someone who has a different faith than you.

Speak not of doleful things at the table;
speak not of melancholy things as death
and wounds, and if others mention them,
change if you can the discourse.
George Washington

Stain Remover

Never dip your fingers or napkin in the water glass to wipe something off your clothes or take ice from your glass to rub on a stained spot. It looks unsanitary to others.

If you have an accident, excuse yourself to the bathroom where you can dab water on the stain in private.

Suggestion: Talk about why this rule is important and about remedies you can employ once you reach the restroom, such as a handy Tide-to-Go Stick® or some other kind of stain remover.

Mrs. Joe was a very clean housekeeper, but had an exquisite art of making her cleanliness more uncomfortable and unacceptable than dirt itself.
Charles Dickens

Cool It

Do not blow on your food to cool it unless you are at home with family. When you are eating out with others, blowing on your food appears juvenile. Simply wait until the food cools to eat it, or eat from the top of each selection to minimize the chances of burning your tongue.

Suggestion: Discuss other reasons why it is bad manners to blow on your food. For instance, you could blow hot soup on someone near you. Practice dipping from across the surface of soup so it will not be as hot as it is farther down in the bowl.

Blow not your broth at table but stay
'til it cools of itself.
George Washington

Shovels Are for Yard Work

Do not shovel your food into your mouth, and do not bend down to meet your plate as you eat. It is unpleasant to others and makes you look juvenile. Always use proper posture at the table, bringing the food up to meet your mouth. Remember to hold your eating utensil in the same hand position you use when holding a pencil.

Suggestion: Practice sitting up straight at the dining table, leaning slightly forward but not down-ward. Work on bringing your food to your mouth without spilling.

No man who is occupied in doing a very difficult thing, and doing it very well, ever loses his self-respect.
George Bernard Shaw

Cloth or Paper?

Do not use your cloth napkin to remove something from your mouth, because if you put the morsel in your napkin and later lift your napkin forgetfully, you may watch the awful thing fall on the table or the floor, embarrassing yourself or others. A paper napkin can be used to take something out of your mouth because you can easily discard it and get a clean one.

Suggestion: Talk about the difference in taking something out of your mouth with a cloth napkin versus a paper napkin. Practice doing so as tastefully and discreetly as possible (not actually removing something from your mouth, just pretending).

In seventeenth century France, napkins were often folded into frogs, fish, boats, chickens, peacocks, and swans. It was a breach of etiquette to unfold these. Other napkins were provided.

Margaret Visser

Breaking Bread

Butter only one bite of roll or pinched-off bread at a time, or butter one half of a biscuit before taking a small bite. If you open your mouth wide enough to take a big chomp out of a dinner roll, you will likely expose your tonsils (or lack thereof).

The bread and butter plate will always be above your forks. (Remember, the salad plate is left of the forks. "Bread" and "butter" both begin with "b," and the word "above" has a "b" in it.)

Suggestion: Practice as you pinch off a bite of roll, buttering that piece and then eating it. If you have a biscuit or a bagel, practice separating the top from the bottom and eating from one at a time. Cornbread may be eaten from the whole because it will crumble if you try to divide it.

♦ ♦ ♦ ♦ ♦ ♦

Good manners will open doors that the best education cannot.
Clarence Thomas

This Can't Be Good

If you find some foreign, unwanted objects in your food, do not announce it to your tablemates. You will spoil their appetites. In a restaurant, quietly ask a waiter to bring you another serving. In someone's home, simply sit and say nothing. If the hostess notices you are not eating, you may ask for another dish. Do not talk about the offending object.

Suggestion: Discuss unpleasant food experiences that family members may have had and how they handled them. Establish a good family rule and practice of not offending someone with something that may have offended you.

One of the greatest victories you can gain over someone is to beat him at politeness.
Josh Billings

Dropping Hints

If you drop a piece of silverware on the floor in a restaurant, never pick it up. Politely ask the waiter to bring you another one. If it is in the walkway where someone might trip over it, move it out of the way with your foot until you can summon a waiter. Never return a dropped piece to the tabletop. In someone's home, you may pick it up and hand it to the hostess, if she comes to you.

Suggestion: Talk about experiences that include dropping something while you eat. How did you handle it, and how should you handle it in the future?

Maître d' is short for maître d'hôtel *in French, which means "master of the house" (or captain or headwaiter).*

Self-Serving

Never use your own piece of silverware to take something from a communal dish of food because you will likely transfer your germs to the platter or the food. Use instead the serving utensil that accompanies the dish.

Suggestion: Practice using the serving pieces in each dish. At home, if there are no pieces in any particular bowl or dish, you should briefly excuse yourself and get some. If you are eating in another's home, kindly ask the hostess if you may please have one. She probably simply overlooked it and will be glad to retrieve one.

Never eat more than you can lift.
Miss Piggy

Mistakes Will Happen

If you drop something on the tablecloth, scoop it up with your spoon or knife and place it on the edge of your plate. Neither you nor others will want to look at the thing.

If you have a major mishap, apologize to the hostess and offer to help clean it up. But do not continue talking about it throughout the remainder of the meal. Move on to something else.

Suggestion: Talk about incidences when family members have accidentally dropped something on the tablecloth or spilled a liquid. At home, you should clean up your own mess and help parents or siblings when they have accidents.

We probably wouldn't worry about what people think of us if we could know how seldom they do.
Olin Miller

Mixed Up

Never mix up food on your plate, stirring or scooting it together, unless it is meant to be mixed in this way. Such a mixed mess or concoction is very unappetizing to other diners. Keep your food in its own serving space on your plate.

Suggestion: Talk about food that can be mixed and foods that should never be. Gravy and mashed potatoes, for example, go together. Onions and applesauce do not. What others can you think of? Also, talk about the importance to other diners of how food is arranged on our plates.

I seek constantly to improve my manners and graces, for they are the sugar to which all are attracted.
Og Mandino

Don't Stuff Yourself

Do not put more food on your fork or spoon than you can eat at one time because you will have to stuff your mouth too full. This is always unpleasant for others to see—not to mention, it may cause you to choke or swallow too big of a bite.

Suggestion: Practice putting only small portions of meat and vegetables on your fork at a time. Practice eating smaller bites so that you do not stuff your mouth. Practice eating smaller spoonfuls of stew. Dining should be enjoyed like a slow walk, not a foot race.

Eat not ravenously, filling the mouth gulp after gulp without breathing space.

Maimonides

This Is a Stick-Up

For safety's sake, never leave a spoon protruding up from a bowl or a glass. If you leave a spoon sticking up in an iced tea glass, you can poke yourself in the eye. And if you bump a soup spoon, you might send it hurtling across the table, taking accidental splashes of food or liquid with it.

Suggestion: Practice placing the soup spoon on the plate beneath it. Also, practice propping the teaspoon with the bowl of the spoon inverted on the rim of a plate. Remember, never place used silverware back on the table.

*In Germany, it is rude to cut potatoes
with a knife, or pancakes, or dumplings.
In Italy, it is never "done" to cut spaghetti.*
Margaret Visser

Last One Standing

Never take the last piece of food from a dish or platter. In fact, it is selfish to reach for the last of anything. If you are a guest, simply say nothing, not bringing attention to the fact that only one of an item is left. But if you are with family or close friends, you may say, "Would someone like to share this last piece of pizza?" (Often the hostess will ask if someone wants the last piece. If you accept, you should still offer to share it.)

Suggestion: Practice offering to share the last piece of something at your next meal together as a family.

Friends share all things.
Pythagoras

Unspoken Requests

To summon a waiter in a restaurant, the head of the group simply catches a waiter's eye and motions for him or her to come to your table. You should never shout or make noise in a restaurant, calling out to someone for service.

Suggestion: Let the younger members of the family be the servers at home, and let family members who are seated practice summoning a waiter. Be kind, remembering that tomorrow night it's your turn to serve and be summoned. Or plan an evening out at any restaurant that has servers or waiters.

*Be kind. Everyone you meet
is fighting a hard battle.*
T. H. Thompson

Undercooked

If you go to a restaurant with the family and you get a bad piece of meat, or if it is not cooked the way you ordered it, Dad (or the host paying the bill) should quietly motion for a server so you can explain the problem.

Remember, the server did not cook the food, but he or she should take it back to the kitchen. Never make a scene, but you may ask for the maitre d' or manager.

Suggestion: Reminisce about times when you as a family member may have wanted to send food back because it was not prepared quite right. Talk about how you might handle it the next time you find yourself in such a position.

The restaurant hostess asks: "Would you like the smoking, cell-phone, parents-of-small-children, opinionated-loudmouth, or nose-blowing section?"
Cartoon quote

When You've Had Enough

Never cover the top of a cup or glass or turn it bottom-side up to show that you are refusing a beverage. This is offensive to the host. Simply say, "No, thank you." (The waiter often takes away the empty glass, and a hostess usually remembers and doesn't offer it to you again.)

It is also rude to ask for another beverage unless the hostess asks for your preference. Just drink your water. In a restaurant, of course, you can order whatever beverage you like.

Suggestion: Practice by politely saying, "No, thank you" when you are offered a beverage you do not drink. Do not make comments.

Drink because you are happy,
but never because you are miserable.
G.K. Chesterton

Speed Zone

It is polite to gauge the speed of your eating with others at the table so you will be able to finish at about the same time—not long before them or long after them. It may even mean, if you find others finishing quickly, that you won't be able to eat everything on your plate before signaling that you're through.

Suggestion: Talk about fast eaters and slow eaters in the family. Help one another gauge the pace of their dining. Be kind.

Recent studies conducted by Harvard University, Stanford Research Institute, and the Carnegie Foundation showed that 85% of our future success depends on social skills.

Fast Finisher

If you find that you are completing your meal ahead of others at the table, do not push your plate back away from you or stack up your dishes to announce that you are finished. Be considerate of slow eaters, not looking annoyed at their slow pace.

Suggestion: Talk about times when you may be tempted to stack up your dishes, such as in a cafeteria setting. Discuss ways to remember this rule and also about pacing your eating speed.

The program for a feast goes by the French name, menu, *which derives from the Latin* minor minutus. *It gives the details of the performance, as do the "minutes" of a meeting.*

Margaret Visser

Clean Your Plate?

It is no longer the rule that you must eat every last morsel on your plate, nor is it necessary to leave just a little of everything on your plate. If you like the food, you may eat all of it, but do not scrape your plate clean. When you feel satisfied, you may leave a little. (Parents, of course, make their own rules about what their children eat.)

Suggestion: Talk about your family's value system regarding eating all your food or leaving a little. Some families require only that everything be tasted.

♦ ♦ ♦ ♦ ♦ ♦ ♦

In eating, a third of the stomach should be filled with food, a third with drink, and the rest left empty.
The Talmud

Sitting Back

When you are resting during your meal, planning to reach for your glass or cup or to use your napkin, place your knife across the top of your plate with the cutting edge toward the center of the plate. Simply lay your fork down anywhere on your plate with the tines pointing upward if you are eating American style. Both handles must rest securely on the plate, with the ends of the handles never resting on the tabletop. Never gangplank your silverware. (Remember, the iced tea spoon is the only piece you can invert and prop.)

Suggestion: Practice laying your silverware on your plate properly when you are simply resting in the middle of your meal. Talk about what it looks like to have your silverware hanging from your plate like oars on a fishing boat.

There is no accomplishment so easy to acquire as politeness, and none more profitable.
George Bernard Shaw

Feet on the Floor

Do not lean back in a chair, resting on the back legs, because this poses several different hazards. The chair might slide out from under you, causing you to fall. The extra pressure on the back legs could cause them to break. Even if not, this is an improper way to sit. Keep all four chair legs on the floor at all times.

Suggestion: Talk about ways to avoid tilting your chair back when tempted. Practice keeping all four legs of the chair on the floor. Give gentle reminders to family members who forget.

Europeans once stood to eat every meal because "they believed that eating food while upright facilitated digestion: to this day Scots like eating their porridge standing up."
Margaret Visser

All Done

When you finish eating in a restaurant, place your knife (blade turned toward center of plate) and fork in a parallel position with the knife above the fork, and both placed securely on the plate in the clocklike position of 3:50 (ten minutes to four), the same as at home (see #299). This is not only the proper position, it is also a silent signal to the waiter or hostess that you have finished that course or have finished your meal.

Suggestion: Practice placing your utensils in the finished position at the end of your meal. When doing this in a restaurant, see if your server recognizes this as a sign to clear away your plate.

Nearly everyone wants at least one outstanding meal a day.
Duncan Hines

After Dinner

Never put a cloth napkin in a soiled or food-laden plate after eating because it could mistakenly be discarded with the food scraps remaining in the plate. Plus, it just looks messy. The proper way of leaving your napkin is to lay it loosely beside your plate. Also, never place used silverware back on the table but return it to your plate.

Suggestion: Practice lifting the fold in your napkin and gently laying it in loose folds on the left side of your plate, with any ugly smudges on the under side so that others do not have to look at the unpleasant sight.

*Everyone is a magnet by default.
We either attract or we repel.*

Anonymous

The Jump on Clean-Up

When the informal, family meal is finished—except for dessert—it is proper to go ahead and remove the dirty dinner plates to the sink or kitchen counter to make eating dessert more pleasant. This makes for a more seemly atmosphere and lightens the load for later.

Suggestion: If not the hostess, designate a family member (or two) to remove the dishes from the table before dessert is served. It is a good idea for family members to take turns with this chore, not always expecting one person to be responsible for it.

*Until the late eighteenth century in Europe,
guests often brought their own spoons as well
as their knives to dinner.*

Margaret Visser

Just Desserts

You will sometimes find the dessert fork and spoon directly above the charger or dinner plate because there is a rule that says no more than a total of three spoons, or three forks, or three knives can be placed along either side of the plate. Therefore, the dessert pieces are placed above your place setting from the beginning, but the dessert on its own plate will be brought after dinner and placed directly on the table.

Suggestion: For future use, practice setting the table with the dessert fork and knife above the plate. Place the fork directly above the plate with the handle pointing to the left. Place the spoon above the fork with the handle pointing to the right.

Anyone who has never made a mistake has never tried anything new.
Anonymous

Pointed Reminders

When you try to cut into a frozen dessert, it can tend to slide off the dessert plate. You need the handle of the inverted fork (tines downward) in your left hand to anchor the dessert, and the spoon in the right to eat it.

This is why the dessert spoon and fork are often placed on the tabletop above the place setting. The fork handle points horizontally to the left hand. Just above the fork, the spoon handle points to the right hand. Each handle points to the hand that will use it—fork in the left, spoon in the right.

Suggestion: Talk about the logical positioning of the dessert spoon and fork, and how this makes them easy to pick up with the corresponding hand.

Always serve too much hot fudge sauce on hot fudge sundaes. It makes people overjoyed, and puts them in your debt.
Judith Olney

Freezing Hold

To eat a frozen dessert, hold the dessert fork in the left hand, tines down, and point it into the center of the dessert to anchor it. Holding the spoon like a pencil in your right hand, scoop a bite while holding the dessert securely with the tines of your fork.

Suggestion: Practice eating a frozen dessert. Almost any dessert can be frozen for practicing at home. Be kind and assist family members who might have trouble maneuvering this technique.

I doubt whether the world holds for anyone
a more soul-stirring surprise than the first
adventure with ice cream.
Heywood Campbell Brown

Soft and Sweet

When you find only a spoon above your plate with the handle pointing to the right, you know you will have a soft dessert, one that can should be easily handled with only one eating utensil.

When you find only a fork above your plate with the handle pointing to the right, you know you will have pie, cake, or something similar.

Suggestion: Talk about desserts you have found difficult to eat. Perhaps you wished for a fork or spoon to help you accomplish the task neatly. Talk about other kinds of complicated desserts, such as baked Alaska.

Until fifty years ago, it used to be the custom to provide a dessert setting—dessert plate, doily, and finger-bowl with flower petals floating in the water.

Margaret Visser

Cheers

Everyone but the one who is being toasted stands up for a toast, if possible. The one being toasted may hold a glass, but he or she should not raise it or touch it to the lips. One does not drink a toast to oneself.

Suggestion: Choose a different guest of honor for each meal, and let the others practice toasting and standing. The guest of honor remains seated. This need not be thought of as something that requires alcohol. Water or even an empty glass is acceptable. Honoring each other is a gift of appreciation, worth, value, and accomplishment.

Long ago a piece of toasted bread was dropped into a glass which was then passed around the table for everyone to drink from in someone's honor. The last person was expected to eat the toast.

Here's a Toast

When someone offers a toast, simply raise whatever glass or cup you have in front of you (even water). You do not have to drink from it. It is impolite not to take part in a toast, if at all possible. If you do not drink from the glass or cup, simply bring it to your lips in a kindly gesture.

Suggestion: Continue your practice of offering toasts to those at the table. The speaker must be brief and must wait his or her turn. The one giving the toast simply stands at his place, raises his glass or cup, and speaks a few words of praise.

Dance as if no one were watching,
Sing as if no one were listening,
And live every day as if it were your last.

Anonymous toast

Good Goes Around

The host offers the first toast. A guest should ask permission of the host before offering one. You may raise an empty glass to join in toasting someone. It is not bad luck or bad manners to toast with water or an empty glass. Toasting can be a nice gesture and does not have to be done with alcohol.

Suggestion: Let the senior family member offer a toast to someone at the table, such as: "I toast Sarah on her academic achievement this semester" or "I toast mom for this fabulous meal."

Fear less, hope more; eat less, chew more; whine less, breathe more; talk less, say more; hate less, love more; and all good things are yours.
Swedish proverb

Tipping Points

When tipping servers in a restaurant, remember that they work mainly for tips and are usually paid below minimum wage. The proper tip for food and beverage served to you at a table is 15 percent. In a very elegant restaurant or for outstanding service in a regular one, the tip should be 20 percent. Err to the side of generosity.

Suggestion: Every family member old enough to pick up the check should know how to figure the tip based on the bill before taxes. (Remember to see if the tip was automatically added by the restaurant, especially for groups of eight or more.) Figure a 15 percent tip by multiplying the bill by 10 percent and then adding half of that to the results. For example, 10 percent of $10.00 is $1.00. Half of that is 50¢. Add 50¢ to the dollar, and you have $1.50.

"Tips" stands for "to insure prompt service."

Time to Go

When the meal is finished, the hostess (or the mom) signals the time to leave the table by placing her napkin loosely on the table to her left. She does not refold the napkin but just leaves it lying freely because it is no longer fresh and clean.

Suggestion: Let each family member practice by lifting the napkin from the top fold that was placed toward their knees and laying it loosely draped on the table to their left.

Long ago, all napkins were cloth, and families did not wash linens as frequently as we do. All family members had their own napkin, which they refolded neatly after each meal or placed in their own napkin ring to use again at the next meal.

Early Exit

Everyone remains seated at the table until everyone has finished eating, unless prior arrangements have been made with a parent (such as ball practice or to study for a test). If for some reason family members have permission and must leave the table, they should always quietly say, "Please, excuse me," and place their napkin on the table, sliding their chair back under the table.

Suggestion: Choose a family member to be excused during or near the end of the meal. Each family member should practice properly leaving the table.

*One cannot think well, love well, sleep well,
if one has not dined well.*
Virginia Woolf

Proper Gentlemen

It is still proper for men to help the ladies exit the table. Some traditions endure for courtesy's sake. Long ago, chairs were very heavy and it usually took a man to move it away from the table for the lady to be seated and then move it back up to the table. Today, thick carpet can still create the same dilemma.

Suggestion: Practice with the gentlemen standing behind each lady's chair. He pulls the empty chair out well away from the table, and the lady slips into the seat from the right side of the chair. She then helps him maneuver it back under the table. To exit the chair, the lady grips the sides and helps pull it back for her to exit to the right.

The art of dining well is no slight art,
the pleasure not a slight pleasure.
Michel de Montaigne

Chairs Back in Place

Always move a chair back under the table after you exit—even in very informal settings like fast-food establishments and church potlucks. It's not uncommon to see this going undone, with chairs littering the aisles and walking paths. But returning your chair to its place will prevent someone from running into it or falling over it.

Suggestion: Practice with each gentleman replacing the chair under the table of the lady he helped. (The lady returns her chair if no one else does.)

Be not angry or sour at table; whatever may happen, put on the cheerful mien, for good humor makes one dish a feast.

A Shaker manual

Part 12
Other Good Manners

*Good manners have much to do with the emotions.
To make them ring true, one must feel them, not
merely exhibit them.*

Amy Vanderbilt

Rules of the Game

Most rules of athletic etiquette are for safety, and they produce good fan conduct as well as good sportsmanship. Family members should learn good sportsmanship at home by playing games together to learn tolerance, patience, and cooperation. Sore losers are no fun and usually have no fun, ruining it for everybody else. Such lessons learned at home will endure.

Suggestion: As a family, plan and play some active outdoor games as well as some indoor games. For instance, play with a ball and/or net outside and play board games inside.

Etiquette is the science of living. It embraces everything. It is the code of sportsmanship and of honor. It is ethics.
Emily Post

Bleacher Behavior

As fans, we should arrive on time, find our seats, and stand only when everyone stands so that the fans behind can see over us. No insults should be shouted at the opposing team or officials. When going for refreshments, fans should take their proper places in the concession line, never pushing and shoving, but advancing slowly with the group.

Suggestion: Talk about displays of sports conduct that you have seen at games—both good and bad. Establish a family value of how your family will conduct themselves at all sports related events.

Sport is a preserver of health.

Hippocrates

Manners as an Art Form

Good manners include education in the fine arts, beginning at home. Children should have the opportunity to experience and learn to enjoy fine music, art, and literature. Such an education will enrich anyone's lifelong experience.

Suggestion: Plan a specific, detailed trip as a family to a museum, art gallery, or exhibit. Rent performances such as *The Nutcracker* on DVD. Read classic children's stories as a family, such as Hans Christian Anderson's "The Ugly Duckling." Go to the children's theatre to see such plays as *Little Women* or *The Secret Garden*. Read good books such as *A Man Called Peter* or *Girl of the Limberlost*.

Art pleases him who gives and him who receives, and thus, like mercy, it is twice blessed.

Erastus

Timed Entry

If you attend an artistic performance that has already begun, do not enter until an usher says you may. Patrons who have purchased expensive tickets and have arrived on time, expecting not to be disturbed, deserve our respect. This kind of courtesy goes for church services, too.

Suggestion: Talk about your family's plan if, for some unavoidable reason, you are late to a performance. For instance, plan to wait in the foyer or the outer hall until you are told you may enter. When you do enter, be careful to say "excuse me," trying not to step on others' feet as you find your seats.

Strict punctuality is perhaps the cheapest virtue which can give force to an otherwise utterly insignificant character.
John F. Boyes

Snap, Crackle, Stop

When you attend an artistic performance, do not hum, fidget, jangle your jewelry, tap your fingers, open or snap purses, jackets, or appointment notebooks. All of these noises and movements are disturbing to others and are very selfish. They distract from the performance at hand and take the other spectators out of the moment.

Suggestion: Talk about performances or events where you have been disturbed by inconsiderate patrons. Also, talk about leaving all noise makers home, if possible. If you must take your cell phone, turn it off or place it on vibrating mode.

Fine art is that in which the hand, the head, and the heart of man go together.
John Ruskin

When to Clap

Important rules about applauding in public keep us from disturbing others while showing respect for the performers.

1) At the ballet, applaud at the conclusion of a dance or a scene. 2) At the symphony, applaud when the conductor or guest soloist walks out onto the stage. 3) Stop clapping when the conductor steps onto the podium and raises his baton. 4) When the conductor turns to face the audience and bows, the patrons applaud for the music.

Suggestion: Look up various types of arts in an encyclopedia or go online to learn the particulars of a performance you plan to attend. See who in the family can name all four of the above rules with its corresponding art.

* . ♦ . . ♦ ♦ . ♦ . ♦ . ♦

Applause waits on success.
Benjamin Franklin

Applause Meters

There is a proper way to applaud. Applause performed incorrectly just sounds like slapping. The sound of clapping should be pleasing to the ear while registering your approval and pleasure toward the performance.

Clap with the fingers of one hand into the palm of the other hand, not palm-to-palm or cupped together, which sounds too boisterous and loud. Do not clap in front of your face. Hands at shoulder level is best. Do not applaud after others have stopped their clapping.

Suggestion: Practice your applause by using the above techniques. See how others are doing.

Unruly manners or ill-timed applause
wrong the best speaker or the justest cause.
Alexander Pope

Seen, Not Heard

There are rules for audience participation in public places. Here are a few: Do not kick the seats in front of you, prop your feet near someone's head, leave your seat repeatedly to go to the concession stand or to the bathroom, talk throughout the movie or the performance, sigh and groan when you approve or disapprove, or sniffle incessantly.

Suggestion: Talk about events you've attended where some or all of these rules were broken. How did it affect your enjoyment of the performance? Decide together on the values you want your family to have.

I have often regretted my speech, never my silence.

Xenocrates

Museum Manners

Even though museums can be enjoyed individually or in a group with a guide, rules are important because you are usually among many people who want to enjoy the exhibit as much as you do. Tips are not necessary in museums, but good conduct and appreciation are.

Suggestion: Memorize this list: Keep your voice low at all times, walk and never run, stay with the family, stay with your group's guide, and don't go wandering off with another group because you like the other guide better. Be careful to read and obey the "Do not touch" signs, and thank the guide when your tour is over.

What we have once enjoyed we can never lose.
All that we love deeply becomes a part of us.
Helen Keller

Pointers on Pointing

Well-mannered people do not point, because it is rude. It makes others uncomfortable. They may think you are pointing at them.

There are a few exceptions, however. When someone asks for directions or you're pointing out a specific object—such as a building or intersection—use all your fingers extended on one hand with the palm facing upward.

Suggestion: Talk about how it makes you feel when you see someone pointing. Teach your children never to point at another person and make a funny remark, such as, "Look at that man with the crooked walk." Practice pointing correctly when pointing is appropriate—fingers extended, palm up. Doesn't that look better?

Instead of pointing a finger,
we should hold out our hand.
Henry Drummond

Special Needs

The proper words used when speaking of people who are physically challenged have changed because people with disabilities want to be treated as much as possible like people who have no limitations. The main point to remember is that people have worth and value despite their special needs. They should be defined by who they are, not what they look or sound like.

Suggestion: Establish your family policy for what to do when you see a person who is disabled. Always think of the person first and then his or her disability. For instance, say, "Mr. Jones has a disability." Do not say, "That crippled man, Mr. Jones." Mention the person's name before the disability.

*If you judge people,
you have no time to love them.*
Mother Teresa

Help Wanted?

It is proper to ask individuals with a disability if and how they would like our help. A comment such as "Oh, let me do that" can perhaps be demeaning. If you see someone in a wheelchair having trouble maneuvering, you should politely ask if that person would like some help, then wait for his answer. Some people with disabilities prefer to do everything themselves, no matter how difficult the task.

Suggestion: Talk about what "demeaning" means. Think of someone you might know who has a disability. Discuss offering assistance.

The word "handicapped" was coined when the British crown gave special caps to disabled veterans of war so they could beg on the street for a living—thus the negative connotation today.

Valuing Diversity

People with one disability do not automatically have others. For instance, a person with a visual impairment may possess a keen ability to hear. Again, this is important to remember because we tend to devalue the handicapped when, in fact, they often possess abilities and attitudes we could all hope to have.

Suggestion: Let different family members pretend to have a disability. For instance, blindfold a family member to pretend to be blind. If you find yourself shouting to the "blind" person, remind yourself that being blind isn't the same as being deaf. If you have a relative with a disability, discuss your attitude toward him or her.

*Once etiquette is fitted to the lock,
it becomes a key to freedom.*
Arthur Schlesinger

Armed for Service

The rule with people who require walking assistance is to offer our arm, because holding onto their arm may cause both of you to fall. Let them be the ones to determine how much or how little assistance they desire you to give.

Suggestion: Practice offering your arm to another family member, pretending they need help. Say, "Would you like to hold my arm as we cross the street?" Help them feel valued in your eyes, not looked down upon as a burden or an unwelcome time delay.

Mark out a straight path for your feet. Then those who follow you, though they are weak and lame, will not stumble and fall but will become strong.

Hebrews 12:13 (NLT)

Family Matters

Parents are teachers by default. The Bible instructs parents to teach their children proper conduct and behavior.

After all, manners were God's idea first. See the Golden Rule (Luke 6:31; Matthew 7:12) for one of the best pictures of this. Children should obey their parents (Ephesians 6:1), modeling the godly example that is set before them.

Suggestion: Make a family plan for being role models for good manners, behavior, and conduct. Talk about words such as "gentle reminders" or letting each member keep his or her own chart that lists good and/or bad manners for one day.

Teach them to your children, talking about them when you sit in your house and when you walk along the road, when you lie down and when you get up.
Deuteronomy 11:19

Let's Talk

It is very good manners to make pleasant conversation with other people, even when we do not feel like being chatty. The Golden Rule specifically applies here. Even if shyness or insecurity causes you to avoid casual conversation, the practice of engaging with other people in social settings makes them feel recognized and appreciated, and it should be our desire to encourage this.

Suggestion: Practice having a conversation at home, asking open-ended questions that call for more than a yes or no answer. For instance, say, "I've known Mary since she came to our church. How do you know her?" Questions like "Are you having fun?" can be answered yes or no, putting a sudden stop to the conversation.

Your speech should always be gracious, seasoned with salt, so that you may know how you should answer each person.
Colossians 4:6

Kill Them with Kindness

Do not return rude for rude. That is, when someone says something rude to you or asks you a rude question, you should ignore them, make a joke about it, or simply change the subject. Oftentimes, they just want to start trouble, trying to get you to behave as badly as they are. Without results or without an audience, they soon turn to something else.

Suggestion: Talk about how to maintain your own self-respect and not stoop to the level someone is trying to drag you.

If your enemy is hungry, feed him. If he is thirsty, give him something to drink. For in so doing you will be heaping fiery coals on his head.
Romans 12:20

When You Don't Know

If you can't remember the correct rule of etiquette to follow, simply take a deep breath and watch to see how others do it.

For example, the U.S. Supreme Court holds a formal dinner for their summer law clerks—a black tie affair. Once when the finger bowl came, a young lawyer picked his up and drank the water. As his eyes became level with the other diners, he realized his gauche mistake. He wanted to die, but survived to tell the story to his children.

Suggestion: Mom or Dad may have some stories of times they felt intimidated or unsure about the proper etiquette. It probably did not seem funny at the time, but these experiences often become funny stories to tell later. Many people have such stories.

For a man by nothing is so well betrayed as by his manners.
Edmund Spenser

31 Days to Good Manners

The following thirty-one selections comprise a "crash course" in the basics of good manners. Simply go to the corresponding numbered entry in the book to find the particular point explained.

1. First Things First #1 – The six S's of
meeting and greeting

2. For Starters #32 – The most important rule
of making introductions

3. Who's This? #56 – Identifying yourself
when placing a phone call

4. **Mind Your Manners** #85 – Becoming an enjoyable, oft-invited guest

5. **Thinking Ahead** #115 – Anticipating the needs of your guests before they arrive

6. **Get Me to the Church on Time** #127 Being punctual for worship

7. **Netiquette** #150 – Being careful about what you write in e-mails

8. **Good Job** # 184 – Being quick to praise, slow to criticize

9. **Display Pieces** #195 – The public nature of good manners

10. Across the Miles #225 – Personal letters are like handwritten hugs

11. Learned Behavior #248 – The essence of good table manners

12. Place Settings #254 – The proper arrangement of plates, glasses, utensils

13. Saying Grace #262 – Beginning your meal with a blessing

14. Soup Spoons #268 – The correct way to eat your soup

15. Dribs and Drabs #270 – Managing your napkin and drinking glass

16. Salad Days #278 – Good options for handling greens and things

17. Chip and Dip #280 – Avoiding double-dipping with your appetizers

18. Pass to the Right #283 – Transporting food around the table

19. One Way or the Other #290 American dining? Or Continental?

20. The Cutting Edge #291 – The proper way to hold your knife and fork

21. American Style #292 – Handling the switch-off with ease

22. Continental Style #297 – Two hands on the job at all times

23. Ten to Four #299 – Finishing each course with grace and class

24. Mouth Closed #302 – Eating neatly, being considerate of other's stomachs

25. Hard Going Down #306 – In case of eating trouble

26. Speaking of Manners #310 – Using utensils for eating, not talking

27. Breaking Bread #317 – Rolls and bagels the right way

28. Self-Serving #320 – Filling your plate for the main course

29. Freezing Hold #339 – The fine art of dessert eating

30. Proper Gentlemen #347 – Helping the ladies with their chairs

31. Special Needs #359 – Showing respect for those with limitations

Index

Use the following list to navigate through the book by subject. The numbers are not page numbers but rather correspond to the numbered entries inside.

Bathroom Manners

Bad breath 208
Being polite 205
Germs 206–207
Grooming 27–28
In church 137
Toiletries 86
Using a towel 102

Church Manners

Bathroom breaks 137
Be on time 127, 138
Dress 129, 131, 145
Funerals 143–146
Greeting 141
Noise 132–133, 135, 140, 144

Rituals with respect 134, 139, 142, 144, 146

Seating 136–137

Showing thanks... 148

Dining Manners

Accidents................................... 285, 313, 319, 321

Allergies 89

American vs. Continental 290, 292–293, 296–299

Asking for seconds.................................... 288–289

Asking for a snack 94

Beverages.............................. 270–277, 304, 328

Commenting on food 96, 301–302, 318, 328

Dessert 337–340

Dining styles 253

Finishing a meal.................334–336, 345–346, 348

Hygiene 307, 309

Inappropriate conversation 311–312

Ladies and gentlemen 251, 347

Missing something? 267, 279

Napkin usage 263–266, 316, 335

Offering help... 90

Passing food.................................. 283–287, 308

Place settings................................... 254–256, 267

Posture 305

Restaurants 258–261, 319, 326–327

Safety 324

Saying grace 262

Seating 251–252, 260, 332–333

Soup 268–269

Stains 313

Standing 5–6, 250

Tipping 344

Toasts 341–343

Waiting for food 249

Guest and Traveling Manners

Accidents 95, 97

Allergies 89

Being agreeable 91, 93

Cleanliness 99, 101–102, 109

Food complaints 96

Gifts 88

House rules 92, 107–108

Offering help 90

Personal items 98–99

Privacy 103

Riding in a car 190–194

Telephone calls 105–106

Thanking the host 112

What to bring 86, 110

Hosting Manners

Anticipating needs 115, 122, 126

Clear instructions 117

Eating 119

Guests go first 123

House rules 116

Introductions 41, 118

Invitations 113–114, 244–245

On the phone 125

Planned activities 120

Meeting and Greeting Manners

Body language 23–24, 30

Dress 22, 25–26

Eye contact 8–9, 20

First impressions 1

Greeting a guest 91–92

In church 141

Introductions 32–49, 53, 118
Odor 31
Remembering names 46–51
Shaking hands 10–15
Six S's 1–20
Smiling 7, 20, 55
Speaking clearly 16–17
Standing 2–6
Using titles 19

Public Manners

Applauding/Clapping 354–355
Bodily functions 198–202
Dress 22, 25–26, 129
Elevators 211–212
Entering Doors 209–212
Eye contact 8–9, 20
Fine arts 351–353, 357
Grooming 27, 195–196
Introductions 54, 168, 204
Making a mistake 170–171, 187
Pointing 358
Riding in a car 190–194

Seating 221

Shaking hands 10–15, 204

Six S's 1–20

Smiling 7, 20, 55

Sports 349–350

Walking 218–220

Speaking Manners

Accepting compliments 173, 185

Apologies 170

Clean language 124, 182

Conversation starters 38, 42, 44, 168, 364

Correcting others 52, 187

Humor 177, 186

Interrupting 100, 178-179

Noise 132–133, 135, 140, 144, 181

Politeness 169–172, 175, 180, 183, 189, 311

Praise 184, 188

Saying hello 91, 168

Six S's 1–20

Speaking clearly 16, 57

Telling the truth 65, 174, 176

Special Needs Manners

Diversity.. 361
Handshakes 13–14
Helping others 360, 362
Proper words/language 359

Technology Manners

Email 151–158, 162–166
Fax machines 160–161
Internet etiquette 149–150, 159

Writing Manners

Addressing envelopes 229, 232–237
Email 151–158, 162–166
Fax machines 160–161
Invitations.............................. 113–114, 244–245
Personal notes.............................. 222–225, 231
Stationery 226
Sympathy notes..................................... 242–243
Thank-you notes 112, 222–223, 227–228

Acknowledgments

I first want to thank my acquisitions editor, Paul Mikos, for wholeheartedly sharing my vision for this book, as well as Matt Stewart—both of whom have been my champions and partners in making ours a more polite society.

David Shepherd, as my publisher, has been and continues to be my anchor since I began with B&H in 1996. (But David's sweet spirit is a lot warmer than an anchor.) Lawrence Kimbrough has been one of the most congenial editors I have worked with. He also has a kind and generous heart toward the good manners that make us better Christian examples. Jeff Godby has most admirably created and designed the inside and outside of the book. I also thank Abe Goolsby, who drew the illustrations.

Without Andrea Dennis as my point person, her team, including Mary Beth Shaw, as well as all the sales staff and the many others whose work I often do not even know about, *Manners Made Easy for the Family* could not have happened. I truly believe that God chose B&H Publishing Group for me six books ago.

I would also like to thank Jakasa Promotions—as well as Andrea Dennis for engaging them—for all their help in getting the word out about *Manners Made Easy for the Family*. Jacqueline and her team truly do a stupendous job, and I greatly appreciate their capable, creative assistance.

As an author, I am grateful to many at B&H who work tirelessly because they all believe that manners were God's idea first and that it is our privilege and responsibility as Christians to live out the commandment Christ gave us in Luke 6:31: Do for others as we would like them to do for us. By God's grace, this book will help us all do that.